CITIES AND MEMORY

CITIES AND MEMORY

Barbara Henning

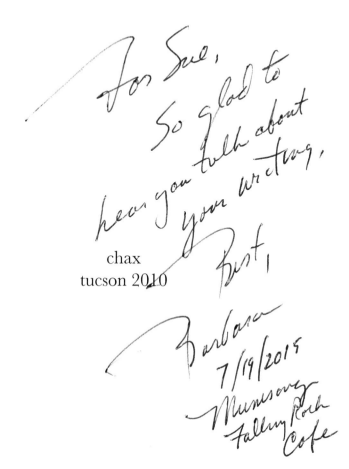

chax
tucson 2010

Copyright © 2010 Barbara Henning. All rights reserved.
Copyright includes all text and images.

ISBN 978 0 925904 87 4

Chax Press / 411 N 7th Ave Ste 103 / Tucson AZ 85705-8388 / USA

Acknowledgements:
Special thanks to Lewis Warsh and Tod Thilleman. Thanks also to all others whose words, images and sounds appear in these poems either by accident or experiment, especially my children, Linnée Snyder and Michah Saperstein, my yoga teacher, Dr. Shankaranarayna Jois of Mysore, Emily Brontë, Roberto Bolano, Leonard Cohen, Marguerite Duras, Walt Whitman, William Blake, Italo Calvino, Lisa Schrempp, Robert Duncan, Emily Dickinson, Louise Bourgeois, Philip Glass, Charles Dickens, Billy Holiday, Harry Mathews, Juliana Sphar, Orson Welles and writers from *The Nation*, *The New York Times* and *The Star of Mysore*. Thanks also to the editors who published these poems and sequences in their magazines and websites: *Talisman*, *Lungfull! Magazine*, *1913 a Journal of Forms*, *Downtown Brooklyn*, *Dispatch Detroit*, *Zen Monster*, *Hanging Loose*, *House Organ*, *Eoagh*, *Jacket Magazine*, *Live Mag*, *Slavery Cyberpoems*, *The Brooklyn Rail*, *Not Enough Night*, *(Re)configurations*, *Flash Forward*, *Imaginary Cities (MOCAD)*, *Cal State San Marcos Community* and *World Series*.

Notes:
Many of these poems and stories were initially published as part of limited run photo-poem pamphlets (Long News, 2003-2009). The prisoner-of-war story in "An Arc Falling into the Bouganvillea" is taken from my Uncles' notebook, Marvel Bakke of Harper Woods, Michigan. The italicized passage in "Bye Bye" comes from Roberto Bolano's *Savage Detectives*, the voice of Joaquin Font.

TABLE OF CONTENTS

Seventh Street	9
The Light is Light	21
Hunger	23
What We Need Now	25
Bye Bye	27
Like a Stairway	31
An Arc Falling into the Bougainvillea	37
Black Grapes	51
Monkey Mind	69
Twirling, the Spirit Flies Off Like A Falcon	75
Little Tesuque	93
Found in the Park	103
Aerial View	115
Cities and Memory	135

SEVENTH STREET

It's 8 pm and dark outside as I walk along Avenue A to the drug store for toothpaste. The man in front of me has two little dogs on leashes. One of them looks at me and I look back until she looks the other way. The man is buying cleaning fluid, sandwich wrap and shampoo. His head is shaved, and covered with a black scarf and he's sweating a lot. I follow him out of the store toward Seventh Street as his dogs pee on every piece of trash left on the street. Just as the man stationed in front of the Korean bodega is preparing to ask me for some change, I look the other way. Then in front of my apartment two guys are going through the trash, and someone has written the word *trouble* over my door. I never unlock the door when I feel unsafe. Nevertheless, tonight I unlock the door and one guy looks me in the eye. Recognizing my hesitation, he says hello with a sinister smile. I nod and lock the door behind me.

☐

Harryette and I have dinner at Mogador, a place where I have eaten hundreds of times. Walking east on St. Marks toward the park, we pass a tall well-dressed black man who nods. I don't remember who he is, but suddenly I think *Pennsylvania*. Then I remember he used to sit in the park for most of the day, and he's from Pennsylvania. We once rescued an abandoned cat together. Someone tied her to a park bench and left her with a bowl of water. We used to talk when I was walking my dog. Pitt, that's it and he's a poet. I'm from Pittsburgh, he said, and people call me Pitt. Later, I'm passing through the park again and someone yells, hey, yoga girl. It's Sammy. There's a kirtan with the Krishnas tonight. For a long time, we practiced yoga together and we both had old dogs and often we'd cross paths in the park.

☐

Brenda has a cute new haircut, bangs and a ponytail. Lee Ann's little toddler clunks past me wearing a pair of her mother's shoes. I'm sitting along the sidewall, talking to a young student from LIU. She's nervous being here. Cliff is on my right. I've never sat along the wall in this direction, he says. Harryette's in the front row, listening attentively as Lorenzo reads, an oxygen tank beside him, a tube in his throat and still cracking jokes. Eleni's in from Colorado. She tells me that I'm looking good. John Godfrey kisses me on the cheek. Hello Barbara, he says as I walk out the door on my way home at 10 pm, past the graveyard—today it's not raining—and I swallow. I will miss the Poetry Project even though I told Lewis last week that I didn't think it would bother me at all.

☐

Birthday dinner at John's house, with Andrea, Sasha, Lewis, and Katt. Lots of talk and eating and presents. Good friends. Then I drop Lewis and Katt off at their apartment on 16th Street and I drive around one block after another for an hour and a half until miraculously an empty place appears on 11th street just east of Avenue A. This guy pulls up in an old blue Chevy, rolls down his window and yells, "Hey, Lady, that's not a parking place." I look around, "It is too," I say and he laughs and turns the corner, continuing his search while I back in and out four or five times and then finally slide in without touching the curb.

☐

In Tompkins Square, a mother with a baby. She's talking on a cell phone, laughing and the baby is pushing her stroller. Just walking along. There's something about New Yorkers that I love. Later sitting at a window table in Madras, I see Miranda coming down Second Avenue. Her hair isn't red anymore! I like it red. Then I'm in a store and I see a little Moroccan glass I like. I'll never find this out West, I think, and so I buy it and put it in a box. When I am cutting through the park, the wind picks up some of the white buds and blows them through the park. I should get my camera. Then I think, I already did that. Come home take down the photos off the wall, put them in a box and before going out for the night, I spackle fifty little holes.

☐

Late at night, driving home from Brooklyn listening to Phillip Glass's *Façade*, a repeating noir melody floating over the tops of a few cars, rain pouring out of the sky and puddles forming in the street. Something is going to happen. Something is going to happen. Nothing ever happens. Nothing ever happens. Something. Nothing ever happens. Just this. Alone in the car with so many rain drops and the windshield wipers going back and forth, and yes, I am leaving New York. But tonight I'm here in this car and the wheels are rolling over the bridge. I turn left on Allen Street. And the rain and the lights in the windows and Phillip Glass's relentless. Nothing. Nothing. Nothing. Something. Maybe Nothing. Maybe something.

☐

Cliff and I take a slow walk to the East River. On the bridge over FDR, we run into Richard Hell, and then we three talk for a few minutes, speculating whether the big investors will figure out a way to take over the projects, too. Sometimes when I'm walking around the East Village alone lately I feel utterly unhappy. What am I doing to myself? I like living here. I like the hip everyone's different and that's ok. I like sitting with my friends at John's place, drinking and arguing about politics, writing and art. Soon though I'm going to pack up and go. There's a rock band playing in the park right now and people walking by the window. Typing away on my computer, I notice some guy chaining his bike to the bars. I'm about ready to knock and yell to let him know someone lives behind this window when I realize that it's Mook. He rode over the bridge from Brooklyn and now he wants his mother to hurry up so we can eat noodles together at the Raman shop on 10th Street.

☐

On the subway, the green florescent lights—sitting here passing time and space with a group of people from various places, speaking many different languages, many silent, waiting together. I cut through Tompkins Square and now it's spring and the trees are lush and green. At Mogador, I chat with the owner. Local in New York City, a place where it's not so easy to be local. The hardware store on the corner where you can find anything you want and we know each other. Driving back from Brooklyn at ten pm—a teenage girl with long black hair stands on the back axle of a bicycle, holding the shoulders of the young man who is peddling. Then they coast down Allen Street. It's dark and the buildings are mostly closed. In the months to come I'll be driving in and out of shopping centers. Maybe I am a fool to quit my job and go traipsing off like this, alone, in an old car with a few dollars in the bank.

☐

Tomorrow is Memorial Day. Will in the health food store says everyone is celebrating murder when we should be fasting instead. Outside the sun is bright and we are like drooping flowers coming back to life. I walk on the sunny side of the street with my arms bare. Musicians are playing drums in the park. See something. Think something. Want to write it down but get caught up and start making mistakes, like dropping a bucket on my toe and the nail is now blue. Like taking out the garbage and letting the door slam, the lock clicks and I am locked outside without a jacket on a cold day. Like walking with Lisa to a yoga class on Wooster Street. Just as we arrive I realize I'm parked on the wrong side. I'll get a ticket. I run home, park it at a broken meter and then I am given two tickets, one for the meter and another because I forgot to get my car inspected. I'm never *this* spacey. Go to meet Lewis for a movie. Afterwards, in Souen, I order a seaweed salad and we begin to talk about our coughs. Suddenly I remember that I left something on the stove simmering. I leap out of my chair and run out of the restaurant, jump into a cab and nervously urge the driver to try to move. Half a block later, I get out and run all the way home, coughing and panting. The tea is still simmering. All is well. I step around the boxes in the living room, open the door and sit down on the stoop. My neighbor Tim stops by and says thanks. And I say, oh that was nothing. Last week he knocked on my door. Barbara, he said, we took our pig Sofia to the vet and now we can't get her to climb the stairs. Can we cut through your apartment to the elevator? Sure, I said and then a ramp and a big fat pig was pushed down into my apartment, honking and squealing. Her nose was squashed into her face and she had scaly pink skin. They pushed her through my living room and kitchen out into the hallway. A group of people gathered around my door. She's not mine, I said, trying to discourage them from coming back later.

I sigh. Tim, guess what—I almost burned down the building today. I'm crazy, I say and he just smiles.

☐

It's extremely gratifying, says the TV newscaster, that someone who was using New York City as a base for a terrorist group is now in custody. On another station, the father tells his son who begs for understanding that he is different from other teenagers because he has Christ in his life. Tomorrow I'll call the cable company and tell them to take the box away. Talk to a friend today who is drunk and repeating herself, talking emphatically about how profound B's grief is. Over and over again. B is grieving. Did you ever go to AA? No, but B did. Lunch today at Angelica's with Bill, Cliff and Merry who is upset about something. Cliff seems on edge, too. I walk through the park and the trees are big and shady. The homeless sit along the outside fence or cluster around the chess tables. The clean and healthy folks are sunbathing in the middle of the park on a patch of green that seems to now be reserved for the well to do.

☐

The weather is hot but I resist turning on the air. Ran off all the copies of the covers for a new pamphlet. Stapled and cut. All done and then I notice the title isn't quite centered. Well, it is what it is. I sit here at the computer and watch the passersby. Here comes someone on a cell phone, with hairy legs, wearing sandals. We want to get an air conditioner. *Hey man. It's so hot. How much is an AC cost? I think fifty sixty bucks at Kmart's.* A man and a woman, young, white skin, high heels. A guy with a limp, wearing black sneakers and levis, dragging something on the ground. I think it's a bag of cans. Someone's going through the garbage. *I did not. . I never say that…* Two girls in skirts and a very fast paced man dressed all in black. A bicycle rolls by. Six sets of legs, three going one way and three the other, bare legs, sneakers, someone mumbling too fast to catch. Now just the sound of birds and the rustle of leaves.

☐

This morning I eat two French croissants, sitting in Tompkins Square, feeding scraps to the pigeons. They cluster around me and I watch the punk couple across from me talking to each other, softer and less on the edge than the punks used to be. Then I go to school in Brooklyn, standing under an umbrella talking to a psychology professor who is surprised I don't want to stay at LIU for my entire life. Why isn't the computer working? Overloaded. It's thundering now. I like this. When the sun comes out, I ride my bike over to Organic Avenue to buy some chia seeds, down Avenue A across Houston and then coasting toward Canal Street. I feel exuberant and happy inside my body, peddling in the sun, 90 degrees with just a tee shirt and no bra.

☐

Helicopter sound overhead. That started with 9/11. Sunday is a good day to sit here by the window. A quiet step, front foot, toe first, pink pedal pushers, clean white dainty sneakers. *I wish you had a stroller for me, the dog has a stroller.* A family in colorful sundresses. I see the edge of the dresses and a man in white pants. A little girl is crying but I can't see her. A car, a taxi, another taxi, whoosh, some leaves and seeds spray up in the air. A little sparrow hops around the tree pecking seeds. She stops and then springs into the air again. Gone. A bicycle. Through the slats of the blinds, a little bit of green from the trees across the street. The blinds are at an angle to get light and see out a little but no one sees in. One blind is up so the basil plants receive sunlight. I'm going to eat them soon and stop thinking about their sunlight. Just enough for one little salad.

☐

Clickity click, two pairs of levis go by, one wearing heels. Some leaves blow down the street, soft from a breeze, not a wind. I hear a child screaming from the playground across the street. A garbage can rattles. I can smell the garbage. The weather is so hot and humid. A stroller goes by. Three giant red golden retrievers on leashes with their owners following. *She's enormous,* someone says. *So,* one black clothed person says to another, and then he cracks his gum. A helicopter is hovering very close to the park. *Hey, this is Howie.* A pink flowery floppy skirt with a little bull dog on a leash stops at my tree. He sniffs and goes on. I peer through the blinds and I almost see the top of the tulips blooming in the park. A pair of green pants and some bare legs with pink flip flops pulling a little suitcase. No talk. It's not the social hour. Oh, beautiful orange sneakers and levis. He quickly stands on his toes and makes a right turn across the street, maybe into the park. A little sparrow hops up on one of the rocks around the tree and sits there for a minute and then hops away. Big baggy levis hanging around some old sneakers. Noisy birds in the locust branches up above. This is their social hour. A darker bird clings to the side of the tree trunk, looking for an insect I think and then it disappears.

☐

Cutting through the park at 8:30 pm, after the rain and things have cooled down, the puddles reflect the trees. Inside I sit by the window and listen. Trousers brush against each other. A siren. On, off, gone. *Yea, yea, catholic spies ... yea, of course.* A foreign language I don't recognize. A horn honks. It's only Thursday, not Friday night. *But naw I'll, I mean even if I.* People are much quieter on weeknights. *I'm on the east side . . . um not bad.* Someone's chaining up a bike to the rail outside my door. Someone spits. Music from a car radio, rap and reverberation. *Nothing, sorry about that.* Quiet step. She stands there for a while. *Hi, it's me, yea it's a one bedroom, wood floors, clean, new bathroom, $2400. I'll have to buy some* *towels, blankets, baskets, some kitchen things, dishpan, etcetera. It's a good deal.* Walk down Avenue A to pick up some oranges from the bodega when suddenly I'm afraid. What if I'm in the middle of Nebraska and the car stops working and I have to buy another car on the road? I'll just have to trust that things will go the way they go and I'll be where I'll be. Very humid outside, almost impossible to breathe.

☐

EZ movers take my things away, charging $1000 more than I was expecting and then asking for a tip. I only have 15 dollars, crumpled up in the bottom of my bag. Now I'm sitting on a box in my apartment with just an inflatable bed and a few suitcases and bags. It's morning and the birds are warbling outside. Usually at night I need fans and air cleaners, white noise to sleep without noticing the people talking and walking by. Even during deepest sleep, I think I am always aware that I am almost never, except in the early morning, alone. I love the birds though. Just outside the window is the sidewalk, then a two foot space with a little square of dirt and a skinny locust tree that leans to the right, toward the east river (three blocks away) and then there are parked cars, the street and Tompkins square with the most beautiful trees in the city, old, full right now, green and in the spring and summer full of birds. Why do the birds come down here? I wonder. I would keep flying over the city, straight into the country. Maybe they were born here and can't imagine living without the exhaust and limited resources. Maybe they like the excitement. Maybe it's the seeds the old people scatter in the morning. Isn't that odd about us, first we are playing with each other, then wildly chasing each other, having babies, working, problems, goals, etcetera, and then we are scattering birdseed in the park, the birds gathering at our feet. Here I sit on a box, looking out the window. Today I like not having too many things.

☐

Early evening on Avenue A under a big umbrella. Big spaced out drops are falling and my cell phone rings. This is now my regular phone. It's my friend Harriette calling from Ann Arbor. How are you? I'm getting ready to leave. The odd thing, I say, is that I suddenly feel as if I don't belong, I don't belong anymore in New York City. Tomorrow morning I leave and I am conscious of the air and the noise outside and the way my apartment was my apartment but now it isn't anymore. It belongs to the landlord. He'll just put a coat of paint on it and turn it over to someone else for a lot more money. Like that. Lots of things in life are like that.

☐

July 1, 2005. Mook meets me in the morning and helps pack my car. Leave a fan and a broom in the apartment, give Stephan the key, kiss Mook goodbye, we'll see each other soon, and then away I drive, taking 7th Street to A to Houston to Westside Highway and up toward the bridge, through the mountains in Pennsylvania, listening to Joan Armatrading. *I'm not the sort of person who falls in and quickly out of love.* I'm overwhelmed with what I have done, leaving like this. For twenty-two years I lived in New York, a city girl, with and without Allen, raising Né and Mook, the immensity of it all, and now a very loud punctuation mark. The children are going where they go and I'm heading out west. Suddenly, I start to cry from loss, no it's not loss—it's relief. I was trapped in a conference room with angry people and in an apartment with no light and now I'm out. I got out. I've escaped. I'm weeping. *How could I break such a heart?* Oh, Allen. Weeping and rolling along I80 across Pennsylvania. They're grown up and this is not about me leaving you again. You've gone on to whatever and wherever we go. In 1983, Anne Urban and I kissed my children and Allen goodbye, and we drove my father's old station wagon with all my things right up to Sally's apartment on 6th Street and B. It seems as if I only blinked my eyes and twenty-two years later here I am, packed up and driving back toward Detroit on the same highway.

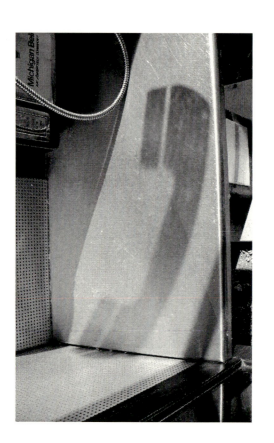

THE LIGHT IS LIGHT

A man wanders around Paris in a long black coat, searching for a woman, while thinking obsessively about Henri LeFebvre's life, an old literary magazine *Luna Park* in his pocket. The pigeons perched on a lamppost and then gone. There's another story I start about a dentist. A few pages later though I begin to drift, put the pen inside the book on the page where I am, set it on the window ledge and my glasses next to it and then I turn off the light. On my left side, then my right, then my left. The light is light. Not drifting off anymore, I stretch out naked on the bed, looking for a woman, the sheet pulled half way over my body. Unless I am naked, I can't sleep, need a stack of books and magazines, too. And then I think about eating something. Maybe later. I think about Dimitri at my desk back in my New York City apartment typing with his back to me. I'm gone from there, too. But then someone reaches around me, turning toward the light, we turn toward each other. I can't see the center of his eyes, but maybe later. A woman behind us on a chair, a puzzle, a pose in a magazine. Two others join with arms and legs. Now I am lying still, longer than before and someone touches me on my arm. How will I sleep at my aunt's house on Friday? I wonder. She's gone, but she lived there for thirty years and after she died, her magazines are still piled in the corner. My suitcase is on the floor, half packed and light. When I'm there I won't think about the emptiness of women carried away and wandering around the house, reclusive and distant, later elegant in her seventies, like an aging model, later forgetting everything. Almost gone when I sat by her side and she reached up and touched me. That's my breast, I said, moving her hand away. *Are you a man?* No a woman, your niece. *Oh shit, I was hoping you were a man.* We both laughed. And then gone. Maybe tomorrow night when I'm sleeping there, I'll wake up and hear the bedroom light click on. *Please help me, help me.* But her bed will be empty and tonight I'm still here in the desert, the sun glowing a rose color through the tunnel of my books and magazines and the swamp cooler chirping like a bird. I call Michah on the phone and talk about maybe coming back to the city. *You won't like the light here,* he says. *I'm in a restaurant on 7th Street and it's raining.* Later when I'm eighty—Wait, don't hang up. Later, much later, will you come for me and carry me home, carry me up the stairs, like a leaf in the palm of your hand, not a heavy woman, just a page torn out of an old literary magazine, carried around in the pocket of a long black coat—she's out so late in the blue early morning light, wandering up and down Fifth Avenue in Brooklyn.

HUNGER

Between Deming and Hatch, tumbleweeds are blowing across the highway and far off into the desert. Big black birds swoop down in front of the window as if pulled into a vacuum created by the car and then they back off, withdrawing upwards. Maybe they are playing with the wind. *You don't let your children play with scorpions do you*, says the deep voice on the car radio. I see a little flash of white wing and then splat, swarms of insects flying into the white pavement and straight into the windshield. Crowds swarming across the mesa. Splat, splat, splat. I pull over. The radio announcer says *Christians should vote for Christians*. And I watch them landing down onto the highway, hugging the pavement. Listening to Leonard Cohen as I slowly drive along, the wheels of the car crunching the insects. Maybe less painful with speed so the car and I begin to accelerate. Later on the interstate, I pull over for gas. Big moths with tiger-marked bodies crushed, splattered and wedged into the grill. Then I'm daydreaming about a new lover, his silver hair, the hair across his chest, Cohen's deep voice echoing in my lungs. Sometimes it's good to wait until the other comes to you, they say, but still I speed along as if caught in the masterpiece. Along the side of the road, an abandoned car and rows of tall crosses, holding electric wires, the energy moving in between, and down the miles, the duplication and continuation. When I swallow I hear an echo and I look over to the side. The buffalos are back, four grazing on the side of the road just outside a tattered kind of middle America looking town. Cattle country, playing country western. A lone brown cow standing on the top of a ridge, a back calf playing underneath her, and the mother's looking out over the plains. A tree a trailer a tree a trailer a tree a trailer a tree a trailer. Train. Mill. Pizza Hut. Down the hill. Elkhart, Kansas. What can you say when you pass through a little town with nothing much and then just as the fog recedes and the world begins to lighten, Dodge City appears looming behind a row of cars, a beef factory in the middle of town and the smell of animal carcasses. *My little darling.* A man left his baby in the backseat while he went down to get some cash out of an ATM machine and someone stole the car. The man was playing a Johnny Cash tune. If anyone knows anything or sees an orange Chevy with a white top, be sure to call the police. They call the side of the road a shoulder here because it doesn't fall off too sharply. On the shoulder of the road there is a rest stop with a line of cars and then a mile or so later, a dead elk, lying on her side, her head twisted back, looking across the highway, eyes glassy, discontinuous. A big black bird is sitting on her back, feasting, his wings rising and falling down as the afternoon moon moves to the left under the cloud cover and we speed by in our cars.

WHAT WE NEED NOW

Did I do something to you? the man on the car radio wonders. *From the start I was hopeful until they held a cigarette to my forehead and then quickly I confessed.* I turn off the radio, pull over to the side of the road, take a left turn into a gas station. Miss, I ask, where can I buy produce? *What's that?* She's reading a gun magazine. I'm standing next to an aisle of beef jerky. You know, fruits and vegetables. The woman is startled. She looks at me like I'm crazy and then tells me to go down that road. *Great stuff at Walmarts, tomatoes and everything.* A man comes into the station, carrying some wood beams while I'm secretly placing little toy soldiers on the shelves with stickers: Bring me home. Bring me home. Then I'm back in the car, swooping down into a valley when the phone rings again. It's Esther. *You won't believe the despair in Kabul. What will they do next? . . . Something's going on outside, the sky is so dark. You just missed a tornado in Kansas. It looks like the end of the world here.* I'm thinking the same thing. Nothing but storms everywhere. The trees are blowing sideways. *I would have called earlier but there wasn't reception.* A big truck is weaving across the road. Oh great, I can't see now, so I pull over. *Don't worry, it will blow over soon.* And then we start to talk about the delicacy of organs, the fragility of human life.

A few days later, I'm on the street in the city in the early morning, the air cold and heavy and I'm talking on my cell phone. In India, I'm saying, there are gangs of bandits who worship Kali, doing blood work for the great goddess. It's hard to keep a loving focus when you're part of a crowd or even a couple. I miss you but I don't want to harm you. The KKK praying and burning simultaneously. Even so I would like to climb inside your shirt, a kind of narrow tunnel. A truck almost hits me, though, like nothing was there when I was standing in the intersection and you laughed. Standing on a corner shivering under helicopters and skyscrapers. I started out this morning with three hoods and a scarf wrapped around my head. I don't see anyone I know and I used to eat out in this restaurant three times a week for twenty years. I order something, but it's not what I used to eat and I don't remember what I should be missing. There isn't anything in the entire country I want to buy now. I'm so tired of buying things. At the next crosswalk, there's a short stocky Chinese woman inside a long down coat with a grey hood tightly drawn around her round face. Excuse me, I say, if I were living here, I'd buy one of those. *Seventy percent,* she says, *that's just what you need.*

BYE BYE

Bye now. Her knees keep giving out on the way back to bed. A B C D E F G. What comes after G? I want a drink of water. She reaches out for my arm, and says, "Mama! Mama, help me! All of a sudden I look up and see her foot come over the edge of the bed. What are you looking for? I'm looking for myself. Please, please—Would you quit rubbing my arm. Would you quit walking so slow. I'm your best secret. I'm dreaming of a cute man. Hell if I know who he is. Who are you? Are you a guy? No? Boo hoo. Sigh. So it's just you and me. Take me away from here. I don't want to ever forget you. I got you babe. Water, please. Where did you come from? When did you grow a beard? She lifts her head up by reaching around and pulling on a handful of gray brittle hair until her head lifts off the pillow. I am alive. I am alive. I'm going to die. I'm going to die. I am a good girl. I am a good girl. Am I a good girl?

The orange sun is hidden in the mist. At first I thought it was the moon. A stack of books on the table. And what do the poet detectives discover, I wonder. *I knew that we were ruled by fate and that we would all drown in the storm, and I knew that only the cleverest, myself certainly not included, would stay afloat much longer.*

A little baby bird fell out of the palm tree in front of the house. The ants are busy devouring it. I'm eating a carrot and watching sparrows and doves pecking here and there, singing or maybe they are complaining but we like the sound so we call it singing. One comes close, backs off, comes closer, approaching the end of the hose, where he finds a few drops of water.

I put elastic bands around my calves to hold up my pants. Pack a little bag. Put on my straw hat. Push it down on my head so the wind doesn't carry it away. Sit upright on my bicycle, adjust my spine and coast down Norris Street, turn right on Third, join a crowd of college students as we cross over Campbell Avenue. My hat is rolled back so I can see. My pants are bunched up around my knees so I can peddle. I am sitting upright. I look over and a twenty-year-old guy leaning against a lamp post is looking at me and laughing.

Outside in the yard in the sun I am holding a load of laundry in my arms, wondering if I can absorb energy like a plant. I remember when I used to open the door of my nyc apartment and look out at Seventh Street and everything was lightly covered with snow. Like a blanket of white across the horizon, not the sea, but a strip of cirrus clouds.

I can feel myself pulled into the computer screen, the skin and effort tightening into a kind of concentration, two deep lines in my forehead above my nose. The train horn is blowing, a mile and a half away. Take a break and peddle in the dark, past the Modern Language building, past the Social Science Building, past a tent with a sign, *Families*. Suddenly the pathway is blocked by an entire marching band with trombones and cheerleaders. I cut around them, feeling my whole body engaged in the cycling. Go past the trombonists, across the avenue into the dark side streets, over the sandy spot and back up my drive. Lock the bike on the porch. Back in the house and it's so quiet. I like it here just like this even though my family is elsewhere. You live your life as a result of past decisions and actions.

Ready for bed, I stop and think, "Didn't I just climb in here a few minutes ago." Blue and gray sleep. Out on the motor boat on Otsego Lake with my father. While he fished, I sat still. The rocking of the boat from the little waves. Looking back at the shore, the tiny dock and the little cabin we had rented for the week.

Fifty-nine on Friday. Yellow flames in San Diego. Wild fires burning down an area as big as New York City.

LIKE A STAIRWAY

The postman pauses in front of the house—big bushy shrubs, a spindly young maple tree, white curtains half opened, peeling grey paint, a wooden screen door and then a darker solid door with a little window. He stands still, searching through his bag and shuffling a few papers and then he passes by, heading up the street. But we cross the street and slip inside the front door, making a sharp left at the foot of the stairs and passing by a Victorian style chair, covered with a dull gold cloth, bronze tacks, the wooden trim painted dark brown, and then a picture window with a young maple and another grey cinderblock house. To the right, a footstool with chipped gray paint, a big brown stuffed chair and a man with very large ears, sound asleep, his shirt unbuttoned and his armpits covered with perspiration. A checkered tie flops over the arm of the chair and half a pack of Pall Malls rests on the table. A fly buzzes around him. He reaches up and brushes it off his cheek, and then he promptly falls asleep. Across from him a low green scratchy couch and an end table. Sit down for a moment. The ashtrays are overflowing. In the corner there is a closet with a low rod for the young children and a higher one for the adults. A tv set and a turntable in a cabinet, painted with a mahogany stain. Three ceramic ducks are flying over the archway to the stairs, first the father, then the mother, then the baby.

A sculpted beige carpet leads into a hallway and a bedroom door with yesterday's clothes on a hook and to the right, a dresser cluttered with loose change and an ashtray. On the pale green wall, two painted girls, light skinned and blonde on a turquoise background, tiny yellow flowers laced in their hair. A low dresser with a mirror, a lace doily, hairpins, a white jewelry box and another pack of cigarettes in a brown paper bag. A wicker rocking chair piled with clothes. And a thin woman asleep in the bed, the blankets rumpled, her head falling back into the pillow like a stairway falling down, down, and then the sound of her almost non existent breath, her young mouth open, behind her a print of Jesus with the little children. The branches of a lilac bush tap against the window, and the woman reaches up and pulls the covers over her shoulders.

Turn around and cut diagonally across the house into the kitchen, painted a deep yellow. An old oak table and four chairs. Two rows of cupboards with cans of soup and vegetables, and stacks of folded bags. A black wall phone in the corner above the milk box, a glass ashtray with cigarette butts covered with red lipstick, an address book on the counter, a white beagle curled up in a warm spot in the corner, and a child in a diaper dropping clothespins inside the furnace door, the rhythm right in tune with the dog's tale thumping and the washer splashing. Out in back, a young girl, maybe ten years old, takes clothes off the line, white sheets in the wind, and the young branches of a pear tree are in the beginning stages of hibernation. A newspaper blows across the yard, resting temporarily at the base of the stairs of another gray cinderblock house.

When the dog turns over, the refrigerator starts to hum and the washer goes into spin. The golden rule is pinned above the door. Go back through the kitchen, past the sleeping man into the hallway. Follow the sound of a ball bouncing against a wall. Red plaid pajamas on the floor, a dresser with a fox hunt on top, three ceramic spaniels and a horse. In the bookshelf, fairy tales, hobby books, *Great Expectations* and the *Favorite Poems of Longfellow*. Big yellow sunflowers on the quilt, a toy fire engine in the corner, and the lone yellow ranger riding his horse across the curtains. The little boy bounces his ball at the wall, boing, back again to the bed, boing, hit a book, back again. Shut the door quietly.

In the bathroom, there's a white sink with pink tiles, water is running, a scale behind the door, four toothbrushes in a ceramic holder, and a girl sitting on the toilet, chanting, I'm three, I'm four, I'm free. Her feet are dangling over the edge. Behind her on the wall is a medicine cabinet with a shaving mug, all spice, a whisker brush, on the wall a razor, an extra bar of soap, pepto bismal, and a tube of toothpaste. A big yellow wicker hamper overflowing with clothes, a scale, a bathtub with three pink rags folded into squares and placed into each corner. The little girl pulls up the stool and climbs on top of a telephone book. Water starts to overflow.

Remember you are not the babysitter. You are not the mother. You are just passing through. Go back through the living room past the migrating ducks and up the staircase, past this and that stashed on shelves—a music box, an old doll, and a green library book. Under the rafters, a closet, crawl throughs, recessed dressers, half built walls, and three beds. A little girl sits on her bed, cross-legged, carefully cutting up Dick and Jane and Sally. Their yellow hair removed, fluttering to the floor, little bits of this and that, a dog, a mother, something is starting to happen. The wind gushes into the room blowing papers all around. A comet, an eclipse, perhaps some star in the evening. A dusty cabinet full of books, an old set of rarely opened Harvard Classics and a worn collection of Dickens' novels. An old painted dressing table with a cloudy mirror. Behind the walls, throw everything, all the scraps, throw the evidence into the darkness behind the walls. Then stand here, right here and look out the window, a panoramic daytime view of the sky and the yellow maple and oak trees, bare branches, and rows of houses, a block-by-block grid growing into the country.

Sometimes when I was a child and sound asleep, I'd climb up on the ledge, survey the horizon and then I'd jump out the window with my book under my arm—my skirt opening like a parachute, I'd land in the back seat of a black Chevy convertible. I remember looking back at the house the last time, at the lilac bush and the grey walls. My driver was wearing a black leather coat, his hair was slicked back—he made a fast u turn at the corner, screeching and then he took me far away—never to return—into the city of dark alleys and hidden stars.

AN ARC FALLING INTO THE BOUGAINVILLEA
for Linnée

Praise then the interruption of our composure
— Robert Duncan

Before waking, I find myself at my father's house, and he's now living on the edge of the ocean. I get into his boat, start it and then go back into the house for something. Turning around and standing at the window, I watch the boat drift out toward the horizon. I have a number to call for help, but every time I punch it into the phone, I screw up and then start over again. Then I drift into something else like right now in the present as I'm typing this while listening to a tape of the sounds in the room where I gave birth to Michah. I am growling and moaning. Little children are running in and out of the room. I hear Allen speaking. I miss him so much. I say to my father—there is something I have to tell you, the boat… I point out to the sea and the boat is drifting back toward the shore, skeletal and charred, stripped of everything. Then it disappears again. And I'm standing here with a little boy body curled up inside a blanket of necessity. Look at our baby, Né Né. I hear my voice on the recording speaking to my daughter.

☐

My uncle's hands are shaking. He hugs me and tells me I am one of his favorite nieces. Then he goes into a drawer and takes out a loose leaf binder. This is for you, some papers about when I was in Germany. On November 13, 1944—I begin to read—in the morning, in the dark, we were told to cross the river and take Bertrange and Imeldange, two small towns. This we did and it took all day. Finally our commander surrendered us so we wouldn't be killed. They gave us one cup of coffee in the morning, one cup of soup at noon and one piece of bread in the evening. They kept us weak so we didn't feel like trying to escape. The one window was covered so it was dark all the time. On Christmas Day, our special meal was a tablespoon of raw hamburger. It was put in our hand and we ate it like a dog. We were heading toward Stalag XIIX, the first camp, and as we passed through towns, the people yelled obscenities and spit at me. For six months, my clothes were never washed. Lice were as common as fleas on dogs. Some men froze to death or had frostbite so extreme they lost their hands or feet. I almost starved to death. One day we were lined up and at random, men were picked out and shot. I stood next to men who were shot in the head and thrown to the side. For some reason they didn't shoot me. Many went crazy, but I kept creating something in my mind, constructing it step by step until it was finished. That's what saved my sanity. . . Now I'm a retired carpenter and a wood carver with five grown children, fifteen grandchildren and twenty-four more.

I look over at him with his head tilted to the side, gazing out the window at the bushes and a little boy passing by on his bicycle. His hands are in his lap shaking. From where I am sitting, scraps of left over food on a plate and through the window the visible sun.

☐

Behind me on the plane, the young man keeps talking—I just got back from one tour of duty in Iraq and I'm going back again. Going to Detroit to pick up a red Mustang, brand new with black interior, black hubcaps. Wow. His friend is going to photograph him in every possible position with this car. He goes on and on in a high-pitched voice. Maybe he's going back to Iraq to make the money for the car. Some of my students enlisted in order to pay for their college education. I put in my earplugs and listen to Leonard Cohen. I've seen the future and it is murder. The law lays down broken limbs and self knowledge.

Cities and Memory

☐

On my knees in Jean's garden, planting some little orange flowers. Spread the dirt with my hands, patting, then watering. Never gardened before. Slugs aren't good for the plants, she says, smearing a little spider across her pants.

☐

This week the sun has begun to repeat itself, creating ghostly reflections on the left and right. Rays of light passing through crystals of ice. A sure sign of a coming storm.

☐

Driving through the Cass Corridor in Detroit. Abandoned buildings, down and out people in tattered clothing, unfocused eyes. Big empty lots. Allen ran an after hours club down here in the late '70s. *The curtains in the window are moving.* A red SUV pulls beside me with four young teenagers waving and making faces—they don't know me and they hate me. I turn right, trying to lose them, but they continue to follow me, bumping into my car at a stoplight. Turning onto I-94, I join a traffic jam and the teenagers continue driving along the service drive toward the casino. A chance encounter, an old grievance.

☐

Back in Tucson, I pick up my dance shoes and drive over to the Methodist Church for a contra dance lesson. Suddenly a man appears in front of me and his blue eyes fasten on mine so I don't twirl away. You're here and then you're gone in the arms of another. As if spring has arrived. Over and over again. Breaking away. Unexpectedly a little pebble is thrown from a truck's wheel and it hits my windshield, cracking it down the middle. A big heavy bear coat with a hole in the elbow. The caller yells out—hey you in the striped shirt, keep eye contact, out there under the moon, so you don't get dizzy.

□

Mike calls Michah from the hospital and asks him to paint his bedroom dove grey. He doesn't want to die in a yellow room. *What soil. . . What Ditch . . .*

□

The last time I saw John was when I climbed into the van with Harriette and I looked back. He was standing in the driveway, waving goodbye to his wife and boys. Fifteen years later, I meet him for lunch at Pico de Gallo, a little joint on the south side of Tucson. At last you have come, my friend. He walks in, thin, erect, fragile, wearing a white hat. He smiles. A familiar light. Hallelujah. I'm seventy, he says. Hallelujah.

□

In Lisa's bedroom, we are eating popcorn and watching *Harold and Maude*, a story about a young man who falls in love with a quirky, honest, crazy loving-life old woman. Who needs thunderstorms when the skin and I stand.

□

Walking Dallas and Choko this morning on the shady side of the street. We pass a homeless man with a shopping cart full of cans, looking just like some of the guys in nyc. Nice dogs, he says. Later outside the health food market, a woman stops me. She is wearing dirty bermuda

Cities and Memory

shorts, black boots, white socks, overly tan, eyes unfocused. Do you have any spare change? No, not today. Why yesterday and not today, I think to myself, mumbling something about a drug program. We are both unarmed. Under high thin clouds, a voice chatters and chants— for a dollar, only for a dollar.

☐

In Boulder, Miz Mullen is wearing a pink tee shirt and a turquoise bandana tied around her head, reading a philosophic essay on the poet and critic. *Every particular is an immediate happening.* At night we walk home from the Boulderado. Barbara, what were you going to say? I could feel you move toward me and then you went back. I have a raw tickle in my throat from eating cheese and corn and from talking too much. We pass under the locust trees. Three poets in white hats. Which is which? One begins with ideas, one with sound, and one can't stop telling a story. Strange dream yesterday morning. A big white rabbit with a long tail. I'm watching it, losing it, forgetting it, catching the tail and pulling it back. Then on the bus I'm trying to get back to the house to put the rabbit in the right place. Lots of wrong turns. The plants I put into the earth, mother of a million little secrets, are populating like night and day.

☐

The cowboys scare me because they demand obedience. I like jazz swing better—each of us has the possibility of a solo. At dusk, I unravel the hose and water the cacti. So hot that a bunch of kale cooks inside the car in fifteen minutes. Men on tv in a ring beat the hell out of each other. With fear of poverty, it is difficult to live in the poetic order. Lightning. Doves cooing. Palm trees swaying. Mocking birds. If you mock, you will be mocked. Yesterday I tried to remember Louis

Armstrong's name. Four hours passed and suddenly I was humming *What a Wonderful World* and his name popped right into my head along with news of torrential rains, streets flooding and body counts.

☐

Then the sun comes out and the clouds travel quickly somewhere else. I remember cutting through campus once late at night in Detroit, heading over to a boyfriend's house. There was no one outside and it was a cold icy night. Frightened to be out there so late and all alone, I ran as fast as I could until halfway across the mall where I met George in an old tweed overcoat. He wrapped his coat and his arms around me. Then he never came back again. I tell Joanne about some guy I like today and she looks at me and says, I really don't understand anything about what you're talking about, this is so out of my realm of understanding. I've slept with two men in my entire life. Both of them asked me to marry them on our first date and to both of them I said yes. When the sky is the sky, it's like a blanket over the desert at night.

☐

In a yoga class in down dog. *Om nama shivaya*. On one leg, the other parallel to the floor and one hand on the floor and one pointing to the ceiling, flying, breathing. Down into child's pose and suddenly the woman's face from *Law and Order* floods my mind. So what if she killed him I think. The sound of a helicopter overhead. Shifting plates under the city. The smell of sulfur. I inhale, concentrating on my breath and rising up into ardachandrasana again. Om nama shivaya. The moon, the tv and me.

☐

Last year during the drought, doves and pigeons were falling over dead in the street from a lack of water. Today, both doors are open and a cool breeze is passing through the house. Then it starts raining, one of those monsoon downpours with giant drops filling up every hole in the yard and the entire street. The trees and bushes are ecstatic. Into or out of. The old woman whose car got stuck in a wash on the far eastside, now a foot and a half into the soil—she's not happy. And in some parts of the country, the water rushes away with all of our technology and our appliances, dishes, spoons, papers, pillows floating off into the bayou. Gambling and lack of direct action always leave us scrambling at the last minute. After the clouds pass into the mountains, I take Anne to physical therapy, old people rolling in and out in wheel chairs, hobbling around with canes and walkers. Thin skin, sores on legs, arms and faces, sleeping in their chairs. Yes, suffering, yes, stink, yes, frightening, but in fact not all that different from a disintegrating butterfly wing or the waves rushing away with our financial woes.

☐

We passed the school where children strove. At recess—in the ring. Choko dies and within three weeks Dallas turns gray and curls up in a corner of the yard and dies. *Sometimes a day is a mother.* I am looking in the mirror at the lines in my face and I think, I am beautiful, yes, I am beautiful. Dark water in the mouth of the river. Leonard Bernstein was smoking and drinking and conducting at seventy two and he was beautiful. Outside the moon is so bright and the clouds are iridescent, the ring turning to the left and under our feet, the horizon.

☐

A worn out café on a two lane highway in the middle of the desert, a train moving along on my left. Odd the way we still have to move all our material in trucks, planes and trains. Words and sounds over wires and waves, but not other things, like cars, food and furniture. Someday perhaps over a wave, we will be reconstituted in parking lots. A big black bird flies overhead, briefly entering and leaving the space of my windshield. I was so amazed when Linnée was born at home, a new being arriving without ever going through the door. The telephone wires stretch along the road. Two little crosses in the ditch painted white, one with a pink rose tied to it. Dusty wind, now dipping down into Nogal Canyon, coming back to the top of the ridge, to our immediate star, the sun in the east so bright and the wind part of the process, too, oh yes.

☐

Today I am meditating for a young friend, hoping he'll find the strength to stop doing what he's doing. Then I set up the ironing board, turn around, slip over the rug and fall smashing my finger and my head on the cement floor. We are what we are. Sitting in a waiting room, I explain to a young overweight woman who has a beard what electrolysis is. She hobbles out of the chiropractor's office in high heels, her back arched, her stomach swelling over tight pants, and her son hanging on to her hand. I ride my bike back home, coasting around the slippery sand spots and potholes, aiming a narrow beam from a flashlight a foot ahead into the darkness.

☐

Pigeons love to make their homes in the tops of palm trees. Looking for a particular letter written in 1959, I go out in the sun under a wide brimmed straw hat. Under the shadow of the hat, the lemon tree and the tall cactus, I take boxes out of the shed, spread out my files and stacks of paper in the yard, sorting and organizing. There it

is in a little sandwich bag, on faded lined paper, some advice from my mother—Listen more Barbara and say less. Every so often I look up from my book and I'm surprised that I'm living alone, standing around here posing with these tall fleshy cacti.

☐

My landlord Wayne tells me a story about his great grandfather who came here with several children. He was a miner and when his wife died and he was sick too, he sent each child to an orphanage in a different state, in the states where they were born. Then he died and they were scattered. Some eventually went back to Croatia. Twenty years later two of the sisters found each other living a few blocks apart in South Chicago. Why did he send the children so far away from each other? He shrugs his shoulders. No one knows. Later at dusk, I'm in the house and I hear an electric saw. I step into the backyard and watch him leaning over a piece of wood and the light in the sky is pink blue.

☐

Last night or was it the night before. I was with Linnée and she was a little girl. We were in Detroit at Gratiot and Warren waiting for a bus. Actually we were cutting down a side street, trying to get there. Groups of angry young men were gathering on the corners and I was frightened and sweating. I pulled Né close to me, and then I woke up and remembered catching that bus and being frightened because I had lived seventeen years sheltered in a suburb without knowledge of my narrow realm of privilege, but privilege, and the grass blowing like it does everywhere—well some grass is more prolific, others scanty and sometimes there's just a desert of scrubby bushes and miles of empty horizon.

❑

On an old phone message tape, a three year old pleads—Da-ad please call me. Say yes, yes, yes. Please—

Five minutes after the sun rises over the trees in the east, I stand outside in my robe, barefoot, looking into the white morning sun. Om Nama Shivaya. The rays reach out to surround me and I am awake.

❑

Stop by Joanne and Roberto's. They are in their recliners before the big screen, chilling out with glasses of scotch and some chocolates. The date palms drop little orange fruit and the pigeons pick around for dinner. *As if men were birds by chance.* Tony Bennett on the car radio—Bill Evans is dying, he says, and I call him on the phone and Bill says, *Truth and beauty.* That's all that matters.

❑

Genny Kapular carries my big suitcase up to her studio on the 5th floor. Not used to climbing stairs any more, I am huffing and puffing behind her. I look around the room at thirty strong nyc bodies standing on their hands and feet with their bellies facing the ceiling like spiders out under the moon dancing with Louise Bourgeois.

❑

The baby knocks hard on Linnée's ribs from the inside. The shuttle bus driver has dreads and he's playing a Billie Holiday cd as he weaves around the traffic on the Van Wyck. I saw the sun only once this week and that was from the subway car. I gazed at the edge of the circle, the shadow of a tree, and then voom into the tunnel we went.

☐

Harriette talks about her mother. Very frail now and she can't see or hear much. Ninety-eight and just now she's acknowledging that she's old. She still wants the doctor to fix the problems but they aren't fixable. It's unnatural for a young person to keel over from some imbalance, some takeover by a virus or bacteria. Some broken thing. Then we grieve. I have this image of her mother's flesh turning dark brown and peeling off like old bark on a tree. In between Los Alamos and Santa Fe, big white rocks and a vista miles and miles over the cliff on the mountain I'm tracing with my car. In a minute I tell my friend, we'll hit a dead spot and then we'll lose this connection.

☐

The man at the desk decides to lie down for a minute or two before a new guest arrives. The bush beside the door relaxes a little until good fortune brings rain. There is a melody. When the saints come marching in. Today we are aware of the steady regeneration of our cells. The baby's skull is tilted and wedged into the side of his mother's pelvis. With his foot he cracks her rib. When he is finally released into the air, he purses his lips into a perfect O shape. *Om Nama Shivaya.* Linnée's baby is born on the cusp of the winter equinox.

☐

On Speedway and Swan, I am on my knees photographing the driers in the laundromat. A little child is pointing at me. His mother is folding diapers and work pants. A homeless man is pulling rags out of a drier. Then I notice my own shadow in between the tumbling colors. I am tumbling along when a young man asks why I'm taking photos. Didn't you ever enjoy looking into dryers? Yes, he says, but not when anyone else is looking. Then I forget the driers for a minute or two and instead talk with Robert. You look like a yoga teacher, he says. I like you, he says. Here's my card. His birthday is the same day as my son's. His name is the same as my father's. Later I'm at a yoga class and a special teacher is in town with a new girlfriend, younger than my daughter, rolling her eyes when he forgets something. He is very tired as he pulls his long grey hair back into a knot. At night, I turn on the hose and the water leaps up into an arc falling into the bougainvillea. I like knowing someone is on the other side of my wall, wherever you are, whoever you are, and I like improvisation even when I'm sewing a skirt, but when one side ends up longer than the others—like my curtains—well then I think, perhaps I wasn't meant to be a seamstress.

BLACK GRAPES
for my physician

It is good to see you, Isabella says, hugging me and taking away my suitcase. I follow her to the taxi as she walks lopsided, struggling with the big bag. It has wheels on it, I holler, but she doesn't stop. She probably doesn't understand the English word *wheels*.

The driver runs up to help her.

The last time I saw her was in India, her body hidden under a Punjabi suit and her hair in braids like an Indian girl. Today she's wearing a little green sundress and she's as beautiful as ever, but with the addition of a few more wrinkles. Maybe it's the tropical sun. Maybe she's thinking the same when she looks at me–Well, it must be the pollution in New York City. It has been five years since we first met, sitting on the floor in an Indian guru's living room. She was struggling to communicate with him in English as he was trying to extract a payment for yoga lessons. Since I could speak a little Spanish, I offered to help, and after that, we spent two months traveling and practicing yoga together.

Now we drive down the wide highway behind the western hotels that border the ocean, turning up a cobblestone street and climbing the mountain into a barrio of little houses and narrow streets with stray dogs and children playing. Isabella's apartment is on the top floor of a five story building with large windows and doors opening on three sides. It is rustic, sparsely furnished, and you can stand on the veranda and survey the circular horizon of mountains, houses and apartment buildings sloping downward toward the Pacific Ocean where today the setting sun is orange.

I want to live here, I say, as I scan the amazing skyline. It was one below zero when I left my coat with my son in the airport in New York. Standing here, it now feels as if I have been living in a noisy cave, rushing down one dark corridor to another.

It's nice right now, she says, but very hot in the summer.

Do you want to go out to dinner? I'm starving, I say.

I am on a fast. *Soy en ayunas.* Maybe you, too? She holds up a book about Taoism and sex. Eating only grapes, ovas, for seven days will clean the dirt *en su cuerpo.* She makes a circle around her belly with her hands.

Seite dias, solamente ovas? I was kind of looking forward to eating Mexican food, but I was also worried that so much cheese and beans might make my allergies worse.

She places a red and blue woven tablecloth on the outdoor table, we fill a platter with big black seeded grapes, and then we sit down for dinner. A formation of sea birds drifts over the buildings and then leans toward the sea.

No cows here, I say, and we both laugh, remembering numerous encounters with the cows in India.

En las montanas, she shakes her head and points to the mountains. We'll go with Rigaberto on Sunday *en su camión.* That's when we'll start eating some other food again, too.

Camión?

You know, um, big *auto grande* for things. She emphasizes size by holding her hands wide apart along with a gesture of an exaggerated question on her face.

Truck, he has a truck? I say after flipping through my pocket dictionary.

Grapes are one of the sweetest fruits, full of water. Actually these grapes are sweet and sour simultaneously. I slice one in half and examine the design. Four big seeds inside. Even though they are connected to each other in the cluster, each grape is slightly different from the others.

After dinner, we walk down the mountain to the waterfront in the old part of town. We stop at a beach side cafe to drink chamomile tea and watch the sun set behind a steady stream of tourists. Then we climb back up the hill, stopping at a grocery store where we find two tables full of grapes, one fresh and one not so fresh, but considerably cheaper. We fill up a grocery bag with the fresher batch, and then wait in a long line behind an old woman and her two grandchildren who are busy climbing in and out of her cart.

At night I toss and turn, wide awake from the sound of loud Mexican music on the street and my body a little too light from eating only grapes.

In the morning after breakfast, we borrow a car and drive outside town to a beach without any other gringos.

That's the house I want, Isabella says, as I maneuver the car around the steep narrow winding road. There's plenty of room for my yoga studio and for *mi escultura*. She is pointing at a big stone house on the side of a hill.

I'd rather live in something smaller like the little cement houses in the villages, but then I just need space for my computer, desk and books. Isabella needs more room to work on her stone angels and wooden yogis.

We put on our bathing suits, shawls and hats and sit in beach chairs under a large grass roof. A very sweet and handsome waiter brings us tea. There is only one other group in the restaurant and the beach is quite secluded.

I smile at him. I could live with him, I say, and she laughs. He is married with three little children. A very sweet man though.

I want to retire early, marry a young man and get out of New York City, go somewhere, like here, live in a little house near the ocean near you. I'll take care of his children.

What about his wife? She laughs. You and me, we have bad luck with men. She eats five grapes in a row.

What about Rigaberto?

Well, I like him very much, but he has many other lives besides with me—his family, his friends, and his business contacts in Mexico City. He is not with his wife anymore but sometimes they stay in the same house because of his daughter. He is not like me, though, and that is the real reason why I say this is temporary. Very nice, but only for now.

A speedboat passes by the waterfront, pulling a man on a parachute over the water.

On our way back, we swerve around bumps in the road, passing the big hotels again. I look to the left, up the mountain into the barrio. That's my apartment up there, she says. You can't get lost here, just look up to the top.

We keep going for a while, driving inland. Then we turn right and after a few miles we enter a village with a big white Catholic church in the middle. We park and go inside. Jesus' body is hanging on a cross, hand painted and illuminated with blue lights, reminding me of the blue lights my mother put on our Christmas tree. She died in January when I was eleven and the lights were still on the tree. Isabella and I sit in the pews in silence. Outside the stones in the sidewalk take the form of one cross connected to another.

In the morning, I am sitting on a tall stool in lotus pose beside a beautiful bright pink plant, munching on grapes and reading the only English book in the house, on yoga techniques for fasting and cleansing your body. With Kunjal Kriya, you drink eight glasses of salt water and then bring it back up. Not today, but maybe in the spring.

I study the collection of sculptures around the apartment. When we were in India, the sculptors in Mysore welcomed Isabella into their workshop, printed an article in the local newspaper, and held a puja to welcome and celebrate her new work. While they worked day and night doing their cast duty, replicating forms of the Hindu gods and heroes, she came now and then to chip away at a yogi in headstand. Her work is very angular and so geometric that they are almost, but not quite abstract, reflecting some combination of Indian and Mexican aesthetics.

I am so light that I can feel the blood pulsing through my veins. It's almost as if I could fly right through the window. I must be losing about a pound a day. Nevertheless, even though I've left the city and I'm only eating grapes, I'm still sneezing from my allergies. Isabella tells me about a homeopath in town who also does colonics, a Dr. Rivera. We should go see him. It would be very good to do while we are fasting, and it will be quite reasonable for you with your American money.

Don't tell Rigaberto about the grapes or the colonics, though, please, Isabella pleads as she puts some water and iodine into a pan full of grapes. When you see him, don't say a word about any of this. She's wearing a white blouse and a hot pink mini skirt. Even though it is very warm, I'm still wearing my levis. Maybe if I stayed here long enough, I'd change my style to include shorter skirts and more vibrant colors. After all, I came home from India with my hair in a long braid and wearing baggy clothes. A friend of Isabella's tells me she can always tell when someone comes from New York because we are usually dressed all in black. When Isabella lived in Paris with her husband, she says, she also dressed mostly in black, but her dresses were elegant.

We follow the beach walking in the sand until we come to the Sheraton and then we climb over a ridge of rocks back to the street. The backside of the hotel is a hideous eyesore and the road in and out of town is strewn with big parking lots and transnational chain stores, such as Goodyear and Walmart. Parts of town are old and lovely, but the seascape is monopolized by foreign businesses, hotels and condominiums owned mostly by American and Canadian retirees.

We sit in a little lounge, waiting for the doctor and listening to Ave Maria over the speakers. Magazines about health are carefully arranged on the table. Isabella places her cards in the center, advertising her yoga classes and reike sessions. The receptionist brings us each a tall glass of water, and then Doctor Rivera calls me into his office. He is a very thin, elderly man who was educated in California. He has several diplomas on the wall.

Hello, Miss Henning. How can I help you?

I describe my problem with sneezing and coughing, especially in the morning.

Besides working with homeopathic remedies, I am also a neural therapist. I have studied in Germany as well as California. I will analyze your energy system, using homeopathic remedies as well as injections of anesthetics. Your past experiences often create short circuits in your electrical network, blockages.

In my prana?

Exactly, and I can correct these with the injections. For example the simple removal of a wisdom tooth in someone's past might produce a major blockage in their heart resulting in heart problems. So in this case, we inject some anesthetic into the heart meridian as an adjustment.

I've had two wisdom teeth removed plus other molars when I was young to make room so my teeth could be pulled back with braces.

I am sure I can help you. How long will you be here?

For about a week and a half more.

It would be nice to have more time, but this will be sufficient. Would you like to proceed?

I nod. I'll do anything to try to cure these allergies.

My assistant is going to give you an acupuncture treatment today to prepare you. Then tonight I would like you to make a list of all the ailments you have suffered from in your lifetime, and all the scars left on your body. They leave a trace in your energy system, in your health. Bring the list with you tomorrow.

Isabella decides to begin a series of colonics immediately, but I feel too light for that so I take the bus home and curl up in bed with my notebook. Just a list, I think, of one word each. Tonsils. Falling. Knee. Throat. Tubal. Tear. Heart. Shoulders. Cough. Wisdom. Mouth. Knees. Sacrum. Temple. That's a life in 14 words.

The next day, I sit across from the doctor's big wooden desk as he jots down notes in my file.

When I was a little girl I had tonsillitis many times, I tell him. At age six I was taken to the hospital overnight to have my tonsils removed.

Were you unhappy?

Yes, I remember crying a lot when I was left alone in the hospital room at night with the shiny steel rail and the white sheets. I remember having a very sore throat afterwards and my mother making me pea soup. As I grew up I had bronchitis and colds a lot. Perhaps that had something to do with the cold climate in Detroit, and the fact that I grew up eating such terrible food.

What type of food did you eat?

Fried chicken, hamburgers, potatoes and canned vegetables. Hardly ever any fresh vegetables. Bean sandwiches on white bread. That was lunch when my father couldn't afford bologna. The standard diet of working class mid America during the fifties and sixties. If I had grown up in the tropics, maybe I would have been luckier.

He looks up at me and shakes his head. Go on.

When I was in my early twenties, a doctor gave me some antibiotics for a sore throat. The sore throat never went away, and I became very ill, running a high fever. The doctors used to give us penicillin when I was a child with the same frequency that the cashier in the grocery store gave us a sucker. So my boyfriend took me to the emergency room and I was admitted. They drew a lot of blood and gave me massive doses of penicillin. Then it was determined I was allergic to penicillin. They tapped my spine to try to determine what was wrong with me. I remember my father and sister standing beside me, very concerned. Perhaps I had rheumatic fever. My heart didn't sound right to the doctor, but in the following year, I was pronounced completely healthy. While I was in the hospital, though, my boyfriend found a new girlfriend, and I was heart broken. I had to move out of his apartment.

Did you ever smoke cigarettes?

Yes, I was addicted to nicotine. For about ten years, I smoked three packs a day.

That means you would put out and light up a minute later?

I quit smoking when I was pregnant with my daughter, but I was always around a lot of smokers.

Isabella's boyfriend chain smokes and he's an alcoholic, she says, but he doesn't admit it. He has a case of vodka and a couple of bottles of wine stored in her apartment. She tells me that her biggest scar is in her mouth. When she was seventeen, she had a job as a secretary and she was making enough money so she decided to fix her teeth. One tooth was slightly in front of the others and she wanted so much to be pretty that she let a dentist pull out all her front teeth and put in implants. It was the biggest mistake she ever made. Maybe Dr. Rivera will want to inject morphine into her mouth. No, she says, shaking her head. Never.

How many pregnancies? He looks over his glasses. Four pregnancies, two babies and two abortions. There must be a scar where my vagina tore when the last one was born. After that sometime in 1979, I had an operation in a hospital in Detroit. I was taken into the operating room in the morning, sedated, turned upside down while the doctor cut a little hole in my belly to stop the flow of eggs into my uterus. I woke up, vomiting and crunched over in pain. A little trail of sutures was left behind in my navel. Then my husband and I were fighting because I didn't want to circumcise the baby, and I became allergic to deodorant, breaking out in an awful rash under my arms. I think maybe that's when I became sensitive to aluminum. Or perhaps it was the stress.

The doctor looks at me and scribbles something in his notebook. Take off all your clothes and lie down on the table under this sheet. He injects small amounts of anesthesia in my neck, inside my mouth near the back of my throat, into my chest, in my navel and then in

the outside of my vagina. He promises that this procedure that is very popular in Germany will somehow interact with my energy system and counteract the negative effects of the scars from these events.

I catch a bus following the sea until I come to a very upscale condo and a big marina. A few minutes later, in the corner of the studio, I strip off my levis and go immediately into downward facing dog. Isabella is talking very rapidly in Spanish so I watch out of the corner of my eye to try and determine her next move. Every so often she looks over to me, *Pierna*. Lift your leg, Barbara. *Inhalando. Exhalando.* Everyone is looking at me as she tries to help me open my chest. After class, I ask her what she was saying. She told the class that I am very advanced in my practice in some ways, but there is a problem with my shoulders that I am not used to working on. I try to explain to her that it is because I am always leaning over a book, a table or a computer. As a sculptor and a dancer, Isabella apparently doesn't suffer from the same tendency to hunch over. No, your yoga practice is not right for you, she says. Astanga is not good for everyone.

We are still eating grapes for breakfast, lunch and dinner. I chew the seeds slowly and swallow. I think I'm going to stop this fast though because I need to sleep. I wonder about the history of her other ailments. We are not fluent enough in each other's language to carry on a clear and deep conversation. Instead we struggle with words and dictionaries. Sometimes at the border of two languages, it seems as if we are able to talk about what might be the unspeakable. Or perhaps the truth is that after we struggle to communicate we often give up and accept each other with our different ideas, no matter what they might be.

Isabella has shown me several small scars on her face and body where when she was young she had moles removed. I imagine the doctor is attending to these with injections. I know she also had a serious illness when she was a child growing up in Guadalahara, but I don't remember what it was. She is becoming very thin right now from the colonics and the diet of grapes.

I don't have any visible scar from this, I tell the doctor, but I suffered from depression, starting when I was eleven when my mother died and on and off for many years, ending in the mid nineties when I started practicing yoga.

He hesitates and writes for a while in his notebook.

My kneecaps were dislocated in 1999, but after I started practicing yoga, that stopped, too. The worst injury I ever had was a few years ago when I herniated the disk between L5 and S1 while being a little too ambitious with back bending.

When exactly did this happen?

Let's see, I think it was in January 2000. My foot was completely numb. I couldn't stand on my toes.

On the bus, traveling from Isabella's yoga class to the supermarket, we get off and buy a big bag of grapes and some vegetables because we are planning to switch over to vegetables the next day before Rigaberto arrives. I love the narrow streets up and across the mountain, each stone laid beside another so the pavement is somewhat bumpy, but a perfectly effective road, especially if one drives a truck and that is what I'd do if I were to move here, I think. I carefully examine the many gringos in the more modern area as they pass their old age comfortably in the tropics with the help of the Mexican cost of living. Well, maybe, I don't want to join just yet.

Isabella teaches me to lift up my chest and open my shoulders. Wear a push-up bra, she says as I am standing on my head in her living room. It will serve as a reminder. When she lived in France, she worked as a Mexican dancer, twirling her skirt in a Parisian cafe with her shoulders dipping in circles. Perfect training for a yoga teacher. Perhaps in different countries, yoga teachers emphasize different postures based on their cultural background.

What about your cough?

That's why I came to you, to do something about these awful allergies

When did that start?

 In 86, a few years after I arrived in New York, I caught a terrible cold and throat infection, and it never went away.

Let me look at your teeth. He looks into my mouth with a little flashlight. I'm sending you to a dentist. I think if you have the molar with the root canal on the top left removed, you will be much better, but first I want to see an x-ray.

My wisdom teeth and some other molars were removed when I was a teenager to make room for my braces. Are there scars from these events, too, I wonder. Perhaps the injection of novacaine helped to remove the effects of another scar.

Isabella and I both go to the dentist together to have our teeth pulled. Are we crazy? I want to stop sneezing and coughing enough that I decide to sacrifice one tooth. In the last few years I tell him, I've had giardia and numerous Indian bacterial infections. I nearly died from typhoid fever. There is a little scar inside my right knee from falling off a slide when I was seven years old. And on my right temple, from a fall when I was running through the house to get the door bell and I tripped over my backpack and hit the side of the table. My forehead split open. I picked up the baby, called my sister and went to the hospital. The baby was in the waiting room crying for me and so I decided not to have stitches but instead to hold her.

Then there are those scars on my shoulders from my initiation into yoga. The swami in a Vishnu temple in India branded me with a discus and a conch shell.

Did you scream?

Yes, of course. And they laughed at me.

He takes out his needle and pokes me in both shoulders.

They were burning hot and red for a week, I tell him.

He injects a little anesthesia into my temple and my knee.

On the last day with the doctor, there is a new recording of Ave Maria playing, a woman singing so beautifully, soft and windy. It makes me feel melancholic. I often feel abandoned, I tell him, especially with music like this. Must the experience of losing my mother as a child follow me everywhere? He injects a little anesthesia into my scalp. I am dizzy, I say. He tells me to lie down for a while. It is normal with that much anesthesia.

Isabella tells me that her husband who was French never held her at night. Her mother and father still go to sleep in each other's arms. So she had to leave her husband. Now Rigaberto comes over every weekend or so, leaving his other life back in Mexico City. I, on the other hand, don't usually want to be held through the night, just before sleep and after waking and maybe a little in the middle. If someone were to hold me all night, I'd feel as if I were suffocating.

I am in bed with the lights out when I hear Rigaberto's voice in the living room with Isabella. There is the sound of ice cubes in a glass. I sit up, put on my shawl, pin up my hair and step outside to meet him.

Hello, I have heard a lot about you, he says.

And I've heard about you, too, I say, sitting up on a stool at the counter, drinking a glass of water. Isabella tells me he is a kind and generous man even though at times he can be a flirt and that embarrasses her. There are three big paintings propped up against the wall.

What do you think? he asks. I'm taking these to a dealer in Guadalahara for an artist I know.

Let me think about it, I say, because in fact I don't like them at all and I don't want to respond with my first reaction. Some fruit, a woman's back and a lot of turquoise paint.

After climbing and carrying things, I am tired. Sometimes, I feel as fragile as a leaf on its way to becoming dirt. At home my dog is getting so old and her eyes are bleary. We've been together for seventeen years. As I lay on Isabella's sofa, I feel an intense sense of loss for my dog, myself and everyone else who I know I will see again in a week or so, but lose in the coming years.

If I were to move here, I would have my friend Isabella and the sea. Sometimes memories and other familiar material seem more accessible and strange when you distance yourself culturally. I'd find a little place in this barrio or maybe I'd move further away from the sea and the tourists. Everywhere I travel, I think, if I were to move here, but there are several years of work left in New York, so I can postpone all this speculation. At the email station, I check my email and there is one from Jimmy, saying some romantic things. I used to imagine moving to San Francisco and living with him. No, I tell myself, don't respond. We both play with this idea every so often and if one of us responds, the other runs.

There are very tiny ants everywhere in Isabella's apartment or maybe they are termites.

Rigaberto is quite charming, but today when we are eating lunch and dinner, he interrogates me about my vegetarianism. You never even have *fish*? Why is it that so many meat eaters are defensive when eating with vegetarians? He also keeps saying he is not an alcoholic, but he seems to drink day and night.

On the airplane here, a salesman for a popular makeup company told me that Mexico is their biggest market in the world. Isabella keeps trying to get me to add color to my face. Some lipstick on your cheeks, a little please. I never wear makeup though. I'd feel claustrophobic with my pores blocked like that. My feet look kind of ordinary in these utilitarian sandals. The leaves scatter a path toward the shoes lined up outside the shop so I follow them and buy a pair of hand made sandals with a loop of leather to go around the toe and ankle. At home, I paint my toenails purple.

The next day we drive into the mountains in Rigaberto's old pickup truck, deep into the country, sort of dry and parched looking land, but still country like country anywhere. We stop at a puddle of water and stones and make funny shapes with our shadows

In the forest, he pulls over to the side of the road so I can photograph a plant with great big thorns. The first form of vegetable protection, he says. He and I enjoy discussing the various ways of saying everything in Spanish and then in English. He is quite fluent with English. I sit in the truck with my dictionary open on my lap. Rigaberto has to stop every so often and fix something under the hood. I have a fantasy about quitting my job, buying an old pickup truck and moving to Mexico. Could I bring my dog here? I ask.

Definitely, you can bring everything to Mexico. We can't go to *Los Estados Unidos* so easily, but you can come here. He stops so I can photograph a cow along the side of the road. Unlike the cows in India, she is frightened by me. When I look into her eyes, she quickly turns and gallops up a ridge to escape us. I guess she knows that here most humans eat cows. I feel badly as if in my glee to communicate with her and to photograph her, I have committed a violent act.

You're lucky she didn't attack you, Rigaberto says.

I sneeze two times.

Isabella picks up a gigantic dried crumpled fallen leaf and holds it over me as my umbrella. We sit on the side of the road on some rubble, looking up in the trees at some orchids. Orchids are parasites, Rigaberto tells us, and he talks about some other trees—I've forgotten the name—with deep brownish red trunks. You can cut these down and put them into soil or water and they will grow again. We make fences from them and trees grow again from the posts.

I sneeze again.

You must be allergic to something here, he says as I blow my nose, laughing and revealing a little gap in my smile.

Stop, hey, look up at that funny lonely looking tree, Barbara. It looks like a little tuft of hair on a bald head. He needs a hair dresser, badly. Get a photo, Isabella says, and so I do.

MONKEY MIND

I am sitting on the roof looking over the rail at the bobbing heads of the passersby and at a line of big red ants following each other out of their nest and down the rail. And then over the top of the roof out across the field, three squirrels travel in the opposite direction. To my right a moving shadow on the wall and then another and then another—the monkeys traveling from roof to roof

A large hawk sails through the sky. Coasting down, she lands on a branch, spreads out her wings as if they are too large for her and then draws them up, methodically folding them around her body. Then the hawk turns toward her nest. She dips her head forward and up. The tone is set by our attention. Minutes later she rises, flies above the trees in the middle of a circle of hawks. Now a little squirrel looking like a chipmunk rustles up and down the tree. The branches and leaves help her hide from predators. When the baby birds fly out of the nest, it is empty. I am behind their tree and behind the sun, observing the economic and spiritual benefit of three chickens and a rooster pecking around for seeds on the ground.

In the Sanskrit *shala*, the young British man with the long nose and high cheekbones bows to his guru. A Brahmin is someone who acts like a Brahmin is a guru is a Muslim is someone one who acts like a Muslim is ahead of an American who acts like an American. Sometimes the left is the right and a thief is someone who acts like a thief pushing through the pipes with the big carpenter bees.

When a flying roach crawls into my hair, I can't sleep for several nights.

A mound of garbage is burning outside my window. I take an old torn shawl and throw it into the flames.

Start over again.

A Texan woman has lived in Mysore for thirty years behind a nine-foot wall. There's a lot of quiet talk among the neighbors about her sexual preferences and how she disappears at night into the villages. She's quite large and moves slowly on her scooter, talking as she drives. I like being a passenger on the back out here in the country, something stable about the slowness and her big back. No one talks about it, she says, wife swapping, prostitution, everything goes on here, everything, even for the Godmen, especially for them.

It's *Pongal* day and I'm leaning over a bucket, pouring hot water over my head. Outside on the street, swaying cows are adorned with flowers and their skin is painted yellow with turmeric.

A bowl of oil and tumeric rubbed into my facial bones. And then I go outside into the world yellow and blurry. On the scooter, my hair is wet and my body is cold and shivering. I hear whispering, the way a virus talks as it burrows under the skin on your forehead.

I'm meditating and I can hear my guru walking in and out of the room, standing there, looking at me. I can hear him breathing and eating something crunchy.

The American talks about how she used to slip her father her babysitting money so he could use it for the movies. He disappeared when she was thirteen. Someone hit him with a rock and he died on the street in Newark. Now she is wrapped up in a yellow sari, lying on her side napping and reading novels and memoirs about daughters and fathers.

My landlady brings me a cup of yellow rice and some yellow sweets, yellow like the leaves in fall.

It is good to have mercy without showing it too much, the teacher advises.

Most nights, the electricity goes out around 7 pm. Slick magazines and billboards with gray fathers and erotic young women. New apartment building construction. Up and out. Brick by brick. The lower caste women kneel in the dirt and form bricks. The young up-and-coming men pass by on their motorcycles, talking into their cell phones. The direction of global outsourcing, India on and off modern. Now we need the ones who spend. Hippies are not of much use anymore.

There is a law that prohibits tourists from plugging in their memory sticks. Only in certain neighborhoods where terrorists are less likely to reside.

On the night of the final celebration, the cows must jump over the fire.

A guru pushes the young woman into a forward bend so rigorously that she must now wear a brace around her neck. Skidding around the corner on her scooter, she falls tearing up her elbow and her shoulder. Her hamstring is damaged but nonetheless she came here to practice yoga and she's going to practice even if it kills her. She lies on the mat weeping.

Don't give money to the beggars, the beautician lectures. They won't even ask me, just you. I know nothing. I go nowhere, just in the house. Ask my husband your questions. I'm tone deaf, says the woman from Seattle chattering on and on about buying some property in Tamil Nadu near her Polish guru and how she likes to be quiet and still after dinner. Melancholic and insecure, the young American has no money and she's looking for a teacher, any teacher who will please answer all her questions and tell her what to do.

We don't know what to eat. The water isn't safe and fresh vegetables must be avoided. Her skin sticks together when she pinches it.

When the Indian man's scooter hits a politician's car, he's told he'll have to pay for the headlights. The guards laughed. Did they know he'd go home and hang himself because he didn't have money for the headlights? The car was a two tone blue and in the air there was a slight smell of exhaust and perfume.

We ask the policeman for directions and he waves his hand across his body. Up we go on Chamundi hill, glancing over the edge at Mysore and India checkered and layered under the sun.

When we pick up the telephone, we're pretty sure there will be a dial tone and when we put our card in the ATM machine, there will most likely be some money to withdraw. Our money is a tool that we sometimes use to solve our problems and answer our questions. The East Coast Swing. One and two and you're right back on the corner where you started. Or was I in front of those two old monkeys swinging branch to branch, and then hanging from their tails, grooming each other. Scratching and dangling and then switching places, the one on the right now on the left. One of them looks at me with conviction and says, "Those in Darfur are suffering because of their own past misdeeds. I don't care about them. Karma explains everything."

At night, I dream I'm with my husband in a flat with many rooms, one opening into another. Please don't leave me, Allen, I say to him. Don't leave me in this room. When I wake up, I realize I am sleeping on a mat on the floor in a room in India and I am afraid.

We speed through the countryside. Beyond the Krishna cows with their long ears, brown and sleek, there is a village with music and the rickshaw horns blaring. I am. I am here. Here I am.

The teacher advises—be careful of these twists of mind. Spend no more than a few minutes thinking and looking into the actual sun. Let it remain a memory. An echo. I am full of doubt on this cloudy day, another and another: I am not this. I am not that. I am on Air India, looking into the external sun for as long as possible. The guru has gone away and I am walking ahead on the path alone, staring into the sun until my eyes are red with questions. And then I bow down to it, bow down low. Don Juan advises Castaneda in his last teaching— *Death is the infallible advisor.* And then he dies.

TWIRLING, THE SPIRIT FLIES OFF LIKE A FALCON

for Rose

Fragile Desert Crust

A fat pigeon puffs up his neck and chases a little dove away from the pan of water. Then he sits on the fence looking away. As she approaches, he swoops down, running and pecking at her back. Away and up and then back again, two together. In Iraq an American soldier studies wood pigeons and F-16s and writes a blog about bird watching. At the top of the telephone pole, a falcon holds a little sparrow and pecks away, pulling out its feathers and tossing them to the side, digging into its breast. Sometimes birds migrate over war zones and the fragile desert crust without casualty oil spills fires toxic leaks shrapnel embedded in a child's eye. Unlocking the little brown cry of the bird. Away we bike, up, into and coasting along, the sun blazing mid sky, a fighter plane passing overhead, the sound of a train's whistle. And then the light changes, pink and cloudy, monsoon coming and going solitary   shake   nighttime   wind   loud and clear

Halfway between Vegas and Phoenix

Just outside of Wikiup, it's 110 degrees in the dark. My brother and I sit on a picnic table, talking about wild animals, mortar rounds in the desert in Iraq, and how the hours slide away after midnight. Then Bob climbs inside his van and I crawl into my pup tent. Tossing and turning slide   away   crawl   the sound of an animal panting outside the tent. Saddam's son kept pet cheetahs, lions and belly dancers. Everywhere humans compete for land and resources. In the book I'm reading a mountain lion carries a girl scout away. In the Baghdad zoo, a lion loses his eye when a grenade is thrown into his shelter. Curled up on my side, naked because it's so hot   slide   away   crawl. Lions like to eat deer. The villagers in Basra are afraid of a strange wild animal brought in by British troops. I drift off into sleep and then wake with a lurch at the sound of a cat yowling and another animal crying   slide away   crawl. In the book, before the little girl goes to sleep, she says to her father, "I am afraid."

I Feel Safe Here

Miles of hills, grass, cattle—cattle, that's the name for herds of cows meant to be slaughtered. Car windows rolled down, hair blowing and the blue sky spreading out around my shoulders. Around the bend a vista of mountains covered with pine trees, the road swerving down into fields of yellow grass. On the Afghan roads, grenades and explosives are casually tossed into passing cars. Two slender deer pose in the middle of the road, long legs and long necks, two together. Nice legs, honey. One of them looks over at me with her ears perked. Last year more than 2,118 Afghan civilians were killed. I am sitting in the car and the black SUV behind me has come to a stop, too. We've been traveling together for fifty miles or so. Two journalists kidnapped in Kandahar. Nurbidi and her lover buried to the waist and then stoned to death. The deer turn around and slowly lope back into the pines. The dervishes in Basra twirl, their long black hair unwinding. Big sculpted shelves on the side of the mountain. I feel safe here   slide   turn   come down   onward   red rock and towering pines. I feel safe here.

Outside Sturgis

Women come here often with their tents, the park manager says. In Afghanistan, three decades of war have left one million widows with only the possibility of prostitution, begging or suicide. The sound of crickets and then I fall asleep deeply. Slide   turn   come down   ring me   onward. Sometimes it's too hot or too cold and the world is full of snow or dust storms or the warlords who control the women and 93 percent of the world's illicit opium. But we need a place to put our computers. Yeah, it's green now but there's been a drought for ten years. Not a soul on this highway at 6:30 am. Then standing in the middle of a herd of cows, I see a man wearing a cowboy hat. With the coming of the ranchers and big herds in Arizona, with the coming of fences and the accumulation of wealth, hunters became raiders. Slide turn   come down   ring me   onward

Lopsided

For her first school picture, I cut Patti's hair lopsided. Our mother had just died. Forty-nine years later we sit on the hill   blowing   a flute   a stick   a sax   When a mother dies, the young children adapt, their personalities taking various forms based on particular gaps. Five thousand orphaned children scavenge the streets in Baghdad alone. On Patti's porch in Marquette, we watch women in white shorts play tennis while Lake Superior winds clank the chimes. Without a house or food to survive. Through the little cluster of forest we walk down hill to the most magnificent blue. The dog races in a circle in and out of the icy water. My cell phone bangs. Magnifies the wetness. Five thousand orphaned children scavenge. A friend's eating a veggie burger right at that moment at B-line in Tucson with my recommendation. And he likes it. And then the connection dies. Why am I here, I think, when I could be there? Because if I were there, I'd be thinking, why am I here when I could be there.

It Just Stood There

Just outside of Baghdad, inside his sleeping bag, a soldier screams when a giant camel spider bites his foot. In Vanderbilt, Michigan, across the pizza aisle a man tells me that a few weeks earlier he saw a bear on the side of the road. It just stood there next to a pine tree   pure elegant   and symmetrical. Just outside of town, I'm wearing my sandals as I photograph stumps, ferns, on and on along the winding path and then I realize I'm not getting anywhere and there is nowhere to go but deeper into the quiet   with the presence of animals   it stays light longer here and then gradually darker and darker. The cold magnifies the darkness. Inside a sleeping bag, sweat jacket and hood, my hands are cold. A phone call wakes me in the middle of the night. I was born into the wrong family, the voice says. Maybe Arizona is a mistake. Bang. I hear his voice darkening. Bang. A sixty-four year old woman sleeps on the beach in Kuwait waiting to be embedded. Zip into the bag, my ear against the pillow, the lightening rod images. In Arizona the sun goes on and off like a giant flood light   pure   elegant and symmetrical

Pension Plans

Heading downstate on I75, the land gets flatter. The Detroit announcer forecasts good weather, 40 degrees cooler than Tucson and I'm excited as if coming home to flat glass space squat. Nearer to downtown, flashy casinos, decrepit bungalows, empty fields and a building where we once lived, now with windows boarded over. Stop at MOCAD, a new generation of tough beat post industrial art flat glass metal and paint. Labor contracts gone overseas. My father's pension from Chrysler safe though, my stepmother says as she hobbles around a wallpaper store with a cane, searching through books for peach colored swans and seashells. In a nursing home out Gratiot Avenue, her friend tells us the food is pretty good. I see yellow flowers in glass vases and broken old people in wheel chairs. I smell shit in every corridor. Of talk and sliding out the door flat glass space squat down. The merchant from Baghdad speaks over the radio—Once your mother or brother or son or daughter is blown into a thousand pieces, then talk to me about reconciliation. Harriette's ninety-nine year old mother is reading a book with a magnifying glass about parallel universes. She holds my hand between her boney warm hands. "Sweetie," she says to me, "You never get old. You always stay the same."

Protestants and Catholics

In a backyard in Warren, Michigan, I'm sitting in a lawn chair eating potato chips when a young girl arrives maybe seventeen in a super tiny mini skirt with a diamond belly button ring and a boyfriend carrying a big boom box. Surprise. A stripper for the father's 60th. The groom's family in Baghdad gives a dowry of a million dinars to the newly wed couple. The skinny belly button girl wraps her legs around the birthday boy's face and the men put money in her panties. The wives sit around smiling and drinking. The price for brides in Iraq went down as the death toll went up. You dance without your number. Watch me in this number wrap around another. Belly dancing is as old as civilization. Milad becomes a dove or a butterfly. The light from the Wolverine game on the overhead television screen cuts across the lawn. Someone whispers—Get the girl's number, and we'll try to reform her. After the war, female teachers in Iraq got a raise and the marriage rates doubled. On the front porch, sitting with the children, I watch the couple drive off counting their money and heading over to another backyard party. We're seven   boom   legs crossed and criss-crossed and that makes a point. Life in an occupied city is not kind. Hand   dust   glass   talk of sliding   in the air. "The problem is you're a Hazaras and I'm a Pushtan." I'm still on the porch when my phone rings and it's my friend sloshed, depressed, and thinking about making love. The problem with you, he says, is you're too literary   glitter-haired girls   twirled gold scarves   belly-button rings. On the way home my passenger (who wouldn't let me shave my legs when I was fourteen) says, "You don't know everything about him. When we went out dancing, he would get up on the stage and dance with the hula girls. And you," she points her finger at me, "you used to take your clothes off in art classes for money." Then we decided to get married.

Just Sign Here

In 2003, Bush made a surprise visit to Baghdad International Airport dining in the Bob Hope Facility. On the airplane, I fall asleep and dream I have a big orange car and it's completely smashed with a broken windshield. The police are on the median, their bodies twining around the car. A rough looking dude with teeth missing and a bandana around his head is sneering like President Bush, and he won't tell me what happened so I can fill out the form for the insurance company. I'm putting diamonds   seven boom   for your security   legs crossed in my pocket, he says. Were you racing with it? I ask. Yes and I went over the median and a big truck hit it and then crushed it. What's your name? Mrs. Bush is impatient. She's wearing a blue dress and holding a clipboard. He's ok. Just sign here with an X. Greg comes to pick me up at JFK, but I am waiting at Laguardia. When the Iraqis took over the Baghdad airport, they dismantled the dining facility. Now there are potted plants and polished floors and the women must cover their heads. I put a bathing cap on and we all go outside to swim in the pool—Michah, Ne, Greg, the baby and me. The Long Island suburban sun is hot and all is well here. But an aggressive plant twists and turns around the shrubs, loose green vines twining into the blue sky.

Dear, oh Dear

It's cold outside and I'm carrying my baby under my coat, but somehow he slips out and all that's left is an empty pillowcase. Is this a dream? I ask my daughter. No Mom. This is real. So we go looking for him, calling and weeping. Maybe he's dead now, lost in the snow, just skin and bones. You mean no one's going to help us. That's that. He's gone. Snow boulders are falling from the sky. I find a pencil so we can fill out a form. And then he walks into the room, all grown up   awake with the light   the quiet magnificent necessity   Later I'm in the dental office, upstairs from where I used to live on 7th Street and Alex is scraping my teeth as I'm looking out the window at a magnificent gnarled tree in Tompkins Square, an aggressive vine twisting up the trunk. Yesterday, an Iraqi baby girl was found hidden beneath a metal sheet in the sweltering sun. Did you know that at Christmas time, five hundred trees were sent by airplane to U.S. soldiers? Dear, oh dear. I miss home, I mumble to Alex as he's is grinding and polishing. "Well, if you ever need a place to stay, you can always put a blow up bed in my office."

Out of Detroit

On the corner of Mack and Alter where my grandmother raised nine children, there's a Rite Aid parking lot. Where I lived in sixty-seven there's an empty lot littered with garbage. I'm heading out, taking I94 west. Just outside of Chicago, two guys on Harleys pass me, one wearing a black cut off teeshirt, with shapely arms and legs at an angle, relaxing back into the speed. Swerve   old camp   after a clip. The other's wearing levis and a black helmet. I'm trying to follow them as they weave in and out of traffic. I pull up alongside the black teeshirt, cigarette pack rolled into his sleeve. My childhood was like a short cigar. These guys are not wallowing in their problems. Here the self begins with a deep inhalation. He passes me again and this time he turns his head, winks, and then hits the gas, swerving into the inside lane. Empty between nine and the law. Ontario plates. I find a pencil behind my ear. Motorcycle accidents have killed more soldiers in the past twelve months than enemy fire. Low head into the traffic and then perhaps into a pillow. After several hours of driving, I set up camp at Shabbdona Fish Preserve State Park a humid, forested campground, full of insects and fishermen. In the morning, an old guy with a long grey beard climbs out of the trailer next to me and walks toward the lake with a clipboard taking notes.

Pancakes

A cafe near Wheatland, Iowa on Highway 30. The place is full of noisy men, farmers I think. I am sitting at the table writing some notes when I notice a couple of men across the room staring at me. Perhaps it's my earrings, too many, or maybe my Indian bag or the tee shirt that keeps slipping over my shoulder. Is my slip a blue rind leaning between nine and the law? Under Taliban rule, a woman must be covered with a thick veil from head to toe. I order pancakes. "Yeah, the blueberries are fresh," the waitress says, "I make 'em myself." She comes back to the table with burnt pancakes, gloppy blue syrup and margarine. I ask if they have butter. She says yeah and brings more margarine. In Afghanistan, if a woman goes outside alone, shows her ankles or shakes a man's hand, she can be beaten or whipped. Out of the corner of my eye, I'm checking out the men. Slumped over and worn out except for one old wizened guy, his face leathery, thin, boney, strong, old enough to be my father. The boom   the knee   the unconscious   Just as I look back at my notebook, the man yells across the room, "Hey, Miss." He's leaning back on his chair, "You're showing your knee." Don't laugh too loud. Step lightly. If she wears nail polish, her fingers can be cut off. I look down. I am unconsciously swinging one leg over the other. Down is enough   the sea of corn   table waiting Mara   I look up at him, pull my skirt over my knee and say, "Well excuse me, sir." Under my breath, I whisper, "I'm just a city girl." In line to pay my bill, with my unwashed campground hair falling over my right eye, I hear his voice booming across the room again and all eyes on me, "Leaving already?" I duck out of the restaurant into the fog and zoom away down the corridor of cornfields on Highway 30. Swerve   old camp after a clip. Yes, sir. Let them eat pancakes.

Cities and Memory

Relocation

Two big daddy long legs from Illinois are camped in a corner of my tent—I catch them in a napkin and release them into their new locale, now residing at Victory Lake Campground in Nebraska. At the camp store, there's a wireless signal so I pick up my email. Dear friends, Kabul looks 1000X better than it did five years ago. Instead of blocks of bombed out buildings, there's new construction, new business opening here and there, but it's the dreariest place imaginable. Next time I want to tell you about the mountains that ring the city. Beautiful and mysterious. Love to all, E.

The Spirit Flies Off

A bird is knocking around in the palm tree out front, maybe building a nest. Sudden wind   trees blowing almost to the ground   raindrops   black sky. The Afghan country roads are lined with red poppies in full bloom. The dervishes in Bazra twirl, their long black hair unwinding. Whose wind   rolls over   beside me. In the corner of my bedroom a fly has a lease on coolness—he's coping, catching it dead. Staple a screen over the bathroom window and still one fly, two mosquitoes and one moth make their way into the house. A black fly aims for my ankle like a hypodermic torpedo. A big black beetle inside the corner of the window. I flick the screen with my finger and he rolls over on his back. When I look away, he's gone   into the cavity   the crack of night   red tulips drooping in a vase. An Afghan farmer can make $10,000 for a few kilos, an enormous amount of postcards. I never felt right with out it, Allen said when he was dying. At night a big palo verde beetle levitates over my bed like a helicopter and then he drops right beside me. I leap up and run into the kitchen to find a plastic container to capture him, but now he's nowhere to be found. Whose wind   rolls over   beside me   twirling   the spirit flies off like a falcon, like a poppy, like a little rock wedged under my hip late at night—the beetle, definitely distraught and dead. Then into the toilet and he starts swimming.

Organ Light

I am thinner in the morning than at night. Organs don't work as well as you grow older. Still I am surprised on this sitting whipping overcast morning. The sky is grey, monsoon going on longer than usual. At night the branches are bending to the ground and a river of water appears in front of the house. Buddhism spread eastward from Afghanistan to China and eventually to Japan. Organ light into the crack of night. The sun comes out. When you are walking along the Tigris, you can see the mosques, the trees and hear the birds talking. I'm sitting on the porch in Tucson holding a clay head Allen made when he was ill. The clay is cracking and rolls of hair are breaking off. Lizards look for cool places in the cracks in the house. I run my finger down his nose into the cavity of his mouth. My neighbor comes out of his house with a plank of wood. He looks at me, I'm sorry Barbara but I need to cut this. The cavity in the sky. And then the saw starts buzzing and I think of Charles Olson as he was leaving Gloucester. Don't look back. Go forward. Early   break   lodge.   Cut   porch   sick   comes night. Afghanistan's dream of reaching the Cricket World Cup is still alive. I kneel and dig a hole and bury Allen under the orange tree.

Desert Views

The palm trees glisten in the sun. On the steps to the fountain, a young woman with a green computer reaches down and scratches her leg. Insects are attracted to water and flesh. In Baghdad, Tammy says, if I wore jeans and a t-shirt on the street, I'd be killed. A man walks past the fountain, talking to a young woman in a green mini skirt—"You asked me to knock on the door, so I did." Abdel-Qader choked his daughter holding his foot on her throat because she spoke to a British soldier on the street. Her mother used to call her Rose. A college girl says to her friend who is reading a book, "I will never survive alone." An old faded peace sign on a lamppost. A vine climbing half way up the leg, the door. I cross the tracks on my bicycle watching the end of the train disappear. 2500 miles from home. And the wind is blowing dust everywhere. I close my eyes for a moment. The dervishes in Basra twirl, their long black hair unwinding. I tie a red bandana over my face and then peddle faster and faster. A man stands on the corner with a blue paper mache mask bobbing on his head, he's looking south for the dark Tucson souls on parade. Then I'm peddling again straight into the wind.

LITTLE TESUQUE

November 4, 2005. Outside the window thousands of cottonwood leaves are falling and accumulating. Across the way, through the bare branches, even at dusk I can now clearly see the white trailer belonging to my neighbor. A husky man—I've seen him outside picking up brush and hauling it across the road, the road leading up to the post office and then left to the highway and the Tesuque reservation. In bed with a hot water bottle keeping my feet warm, outside a half yellow moon and a yellow window in his trailer. I fall asleep with my book and my face under the blanket. As it is now—I prefer it this way.

☐

With my right arm in a sling, I turn the car onto La Huerta Lane, the bumpy dirt road winding down toward the river and my house. Hurt my rotator cup last week lugging suitcases around New York City. This morning an MRI—suffocation with a hammer pounding in my ear, something only Poe could have imagined. Breathe shallow, the nurse said. Oww. Calcium spur impinging, pinching and a piece of cartilage floating, poking. The skeleton inside, the leafless trees outside, and the occasional man or woman living out here so isolated, so quiet, like human saguaros looking out over sterile sands and fields. I stand in front of the window, slowly moving my arm up and down. Then my neighbor passes by his window, a glint of light, a shadow, perhaps to answer the telephone or to take a cover off a pot simmering on the stove. He's on the left and then he disappears. Maybe there's never any center to it. The propane heaters make a hissing noise day and night.

☐

When I wake up in the morning, the light comes through the window, and I'm drunk on the trees and the sunlight. Pour down your warmth, great sun. The brown leaves make a thick blanket over the ground. Over the ridge, the arroyo, Little Tesuque runs downhill, carrying moldy leaves and debris with it, today a stream, perhaps someday in the spring a small river. As I'm climbing up the path, I see him sitting in a lawn chair and we nod to each other. He's not a white man or a black man or Asian. Tan skin with an elegant forehead, perhaps a Native American.

☐

November 27 – Sunday. It snowed last night. Frigid cold. Put on my boots, coat and scarf and walk down to the store. Pain has let up, but my arm will not move. Can't get a hat on my head or a tie in my hair. Spiders in every corner and I can't reach up with the duster to put them outdoors. Move south girl where it is warm. 20 degrees outside. Somewhat warmer inside. Wake up at night and see tree branches, the moon and stars. Wake up in the morning dreaming I am with Allen in an apartment in Brooklyn. I am standing on the street weeping because I have found a new place in Queens. Day come white, or night come black, I was leaving him. Will you please let me return? I beg the landlord.

☐

December 6. So cold I can't walk outside today. Sky wide open blue. Lewis's aunt died this morning. When I pass by a mound of sticks, do I disturb those who are resting? An arctic blast or something like that, not normal this time of year. When I sit on the toilet, I can feel the cold under the floor, coming up through the cracks. A foot of space under the floorboards and then dirt. Tomorrow the winds are supposed to change and the earth, on this spot, will warm. I wait and wait, but my feet feel icy at night so I buy an electric blanket to warm the bed. I dream I am standing in front of a big crowd of people yelling out yoga poses and they will not follow my instructions. They are laughing and talking. I remember clearly that the room was dark.

☐

Three phone calls this morning from Mook, Né and Patti. We scatter family, must be some karmic thing. Take a walk down the river, hopping from one stone to the next, and then deliberately climbing up into the yard with the trailers. I see him raking some leaves, wide shoulders and bushy hair. He goes around the corner of his trailer and I pass through the lot, emerging at the road. Reading Whitman, Robbe-Grillet and a new book by Juliana Spahr, *this connection of everyone with lungs*, day and night, despite our differences, the oxygen we share with the plants and each other. Dead U.S. soldiers, dead Iraquis. Not alone, never alone, and yet this helplessness. Yes, my brother, I'm here. Cross my hands over my chest and doze off. These evenings are all the same, and I won't stay here forever. The house is not insulated and it's too cold in the winter.

☐

Monday December 12. My fingernails are cracking. I put a blanket over the doorway between the kitchen and the mudroom. Warmer. Coughing worse then ever. Sooth! Sooth! Nothing serious, just an inconvenience. I am in better shape than I was when I was twenty. Richard Pryor died this weekend. Some disease finally gets you, he said. On to the brink of harm. Another earthquake and Afghanistan is shaking. Gangs of white redneck Australians are attacking the Lebanese neighbors. Human rot. I worry about being alone too much and about a little cough, but at least mobs of white racists are not chasing me through the streets.

☐

Make an *x* with your shoulder blade, moving diagonally. I can't feel one corner but there is hope. On the way home from the physical therapist, I stop to buy some paper and leave the lights on in the car for the second time today and when I go outside the battery is completely dead. Waiting for a tow truck in the store, then in the cafe talk to Joanne on the cell and she's adamant. She wants me to move to Tucson. Rent a truck, she says. Buy a new battery the man says, sending me to an auto place on Cerrillos where I sit for two hours only to learn that my battery is perfectly fine. No matter which way I turn, a new narrative will unfold. Back home I am sitting in a chair reading Duras's *The Lover.* Stay as long as you'd like. When I look up, I see my neighbor sitting in his chair, too, reading.

☐

The crisscrossing lines of parched trees against a background of blue. The one I want so much. The glass makes a glare and the white curtains turn black. I always drop out, cut short, leave a little too early. My middle name—can't stick around for the end, always going home before the party begins. That's why it was so painful to receive tenure. I crumpled up the letter and tossed it in the garbage. I stop by Penske to find out how much it will cost to rent a truck and move my things from New Mexico to Tucson. Now I am rocking in Mr. Henderson's old rocker from Avery Street in Detroit. The empty boxes are stacked in the garage ready to be packed and moved somewhere. Sang somewhere over the rainbow to my aged aunt on the telephone.

☐

Sunday night. Two-mile walk. For sale. Tire tracks. Even slower. Skid. Invisible fence. Enjoying solitude. But I'm not like this rock where darkness falls, then snow, then sunlight melts it away, but the rock remains. Lonesome love. Stop at the cinema and see *Pride and Prejudice*. She gets Mr. Darby and her sister gets hers, too. All the women in the family are saved from destitute poverty by two love marriages into wealthy families. Love, sex, polite conversation and money in one swoop. Maybe if I stay put, stay here, stay for a year, I'd meet my neighbor and we'd crawl into bed with each other, his stocky body curled around mine.

☐

My physical therapist's brother-in-law had a heart attack in the snow. He was surprised. She saw it in his eyes. He didn't want to die, but he did anyhow. Christmas Eve. Blue lights put me into a Christian melancholic place. I must be still. The trees and my legs and trunk blend together in the ever on-going present. A memory of blue. Decide to be more frugal. Drive into town to buy one screw and end up spending more, a floppy green wool hat and a pair of gloves. Can't save a penny even though I resolve to do so every month. A long break from men and passion and maybe my psyche as well as my body will be completely healed. Or it would never happen again. The water in the world is rising and rearranging things in ways that might seem tragic. We can't see the larger movement because of personal losses.

☐

Hiking down the arroyo. Animal tracks. Water on the rocks, a tinkling sound, like a Japanese haiku. The whistle of the wind, it is not my voice. So quiet. After walking for a while, I become a little frightened—maybe a coyote or a bear. Up the stream a shadow. I stand still on a rock and the shadow turns the corner followed by the man who lives in the trailer. Hello I say. He nods. Beautiful out here isn't it. *As always.* I reach out my hand and he touches it lightly. His eyes are dark brown. *John* he says. Barbara I say. He's leaning against a tree. And then we go on in opposite directions. Unusually heavy rains in the past few months have created a lot of growth and now everything is dry and crunchy except the little stream of water running downstream over the rocks. The vines appear to be choking this tree. The same type is growing up the side of the house. A rail on the side of 73 South and a small white cross.

☐

Behind the fluffy remains of dried plants, his old trailer with one window boarded up. Inside perhaps he is taking a nap. It's cold outside now and if you touch a branch lightly, it will break. 20 degrees and I kick the leaves and the shadows of leaves. It was so dark that night, my stepmother says over the phone, that we had to take a cab home from the shopping center. She never bought anything, just glided the cart up and down the aisles, looking at things. Now she can eat, sleep, it's quiet at night. From my living room in the country to her living room in St. Clair Shores, a telephone connection. At night I hug a pillow in the same way I used to hug my husband. If you want sex, the guru says, get married.

☐

Brown dried leaves hanging off a branch, misty white sky, an elegant haiku, swinging back and forth, outside a thin layer of snow. On the TV, the woman is shocked and surprised and the policeman is definitely

Cities and Memory

concerned. The white settlers kill the animals and the Indians night after night. The Indians look like my neighbors. Their faces enter into my consciousness, my meditation, surely into my dreams. Turn it off. Getting into bed after I've warmed it. So beautiful sliding between the warm sheets, the vines growing into the crevices between the door and doorjamb. You do know it's all over, don't you? the woman says. Uselessly. All night, these voices return.

☐

Something wants to be free in the air, in the woods, over the fields. The red blisters on my nose are sunspots. We feel incomplete and so we pose for the photo. For the Sufi, the divine is hidden but wants to be discovered. In Las Cruces I am visiting with a friend who wants me to move there. I dream that Michah is a baby growing right out of my arms and there is a woman here who is old and in severe pain. The men move her body around roughly without consideration for her condition. In the morning my friend tells me that his mother died in the room where I was sleeping. In the photo, her hair is arranged neatly in a bun. Flying over Alamagordo in a little plane, large layered mountains with no forest cover. Windy and bouncy. The mountains underneath, the sky, the desert, white sands—a plain of calcium dust.

☐

The fields were over grazed and that's why these woody bushes have taken hold. The only thing now is to let the cattle trample them or to carefully burn out the bushes, the ashes re-fertilizing the soil. Then the grass will grow in the stretch of land between the mountains, the fault lines stable today, the rocks, cliffs and hills of lava on the horizon. Yearning for the impossible. A man honks at me. I start up, jerking, and turn the wrong way into the coming traffic. He puts his arm around her. The sun is in the west and the moon is a little white spot on the blue background. All else continuing.

☐

Walking to the dumpster, the leaves crunching under my feet, the peeling wood, the fallen leaf caught in the crevice. The three tenants on this compound are away at work. I stand still next to the largest cottonwood. I am starting to feel as if I belong here, like a pinecone wedged in between the rocks. But that's not what I envision beyond the present moment. The dry wind, I have heard you. After dark, I turn on the engine, but the car won't start. Left the lights on again. I climb the ridge and knock on his door. John looks out with a wedge mark in his forehead. My car won't start. His dark brown eyes. Could you give me a jump? He puts on his hunting jacket. When I turn over the engine, his big old blue Pontiac and my little Honda are facing each other.

☐

It's slowly getting warmer but most of the valley is parched and tangled, not a moment of stillness for a week because I'm writing maniacally as if there is somewhere to go. A thousand warbling echoes. The tire tracks cross on the road making a pattern. The sun is amazing and bright, the air bitter cold. By noon, the cold gives away and the dream dies off. I kept putting the wrong clothes on a child and she's going on stage in a few minutes. I hear someone pounding on the door. It's John with a bag of apples. Someone gave him these. Did I want some? He is self educated, he tells me, he never managed to learn much of anything in school.

☐

Back in a field the other side of the river, I see him practicing tai-chi, slowly, methodically, without his jacket on. It's warm this afternoon. His mother grew up on the pueblo. His father was a Polish farmer from Ohio who had a passion for Nietzsche. On the way out to the car, I look over and he waves. We didn't talk to each other much. The word goodbye is final and superior to all. What could have would have, but it's too solitary and cold here. Look what you ran out on, maybe I'll say to myself later. I drive into town to rent a truck for tomorrow when my son will arrive and we'll pack up all these things, these books and chairs and then drive through the desert, in between the mountain ranges, across the dusty plains, so I can set up daily sociability once again in a little apartment in the city of Tucson.

FOUND IN THE PARK
for Ferne and Bob

When I was six months old my father moved us out of my grandmother's house in the city into the house where I lived until I was eighteen years old. He painted it gray and planted an apple tree, a peach tree, a pear tree, and three other children. My mother hung diapers on the line and planted strawberries along the fence. Across the street, there was a park and a big oak tree. I'd collect the leaves, wax them and put them into books. The young maple tree in our backyard was hit by lightening, leaving a vagina like shape in the middle of the trunk.

▫

To read late at night was forbidden, but it was a pleasure and a relief away from the noisy household and from my mother who was dying and preparing us for life after her death. For hours, I'd curl up with Dickens or the Brontes and then I'd shut the book and fall asleep with the hall light on.

▫

As a young woman, I'd lie under a tree and watch the leaves flicker in the sunlight, so beautiful, so perfect, so temporary. I wrote a haiku in tenth grade about a leaf, slowly twirling down, and the teacher read it out loud to the class as an example of verbal symmetry.

▫

My father was never overtly violent, but he was loud and he had a hard time waking up to a dying wife, four children and tight funds. After a while, I came to identify with the characters in *Wuthering Heights*. They had their ghosts and I had mine, my mother, Ferne wilting, Bob sleeping. Now when I'm in the country, I look at ferns. They darken as the summer progresses.

☐

I'd ride my bicycle beyond our block into the woods, park it, smoke cigarettes and hunt for polliwogs and raspberries. A few years later my father remarried and the tangled woods were leveled and replaced by a neighborhood of brick ranch style homes.

☐

In sixty-seven, I moved into a studio apartment with a Murphy bed on Brooks Street on the East Side of Detroit. If you drive down Dickerson or Gray Street today, thirty-six years later, there is nothing but a vacant lot. Before the riots, it was a thriving neighborhood with a row of old elm trees. Dickerson was the first street in the white section and Gray was the first street in the black section. With my Italian boyfriend, I lived on the little street joining them. Typing and filing, and living out-of-wedlock with a renegade, petty criminal, pool shark. I didn't have a car, I didn't know where I was, and he rarely came home. So I cleaned and waxed the floors and visited with an old woman on the first floor. We'd talk about everyone who had ever lived in the building, all their histories. I lied and told her we were married, but I think she knew I was hiding out from my father, who my sister told me was out looking for me—or perhaps it was my boyfriend—with a gun. Sometimes as I tried to figure out who I belonged to, I'd watch the leaves in the wind or the snow covering the cars. A leaf falls to the ground or blows across the street, but in the spot where it lands, everything is in balance, as it is meant to be.

☐

I rented a dark, furnished apartment a few blocks away so my father would think I was living there alone, but I never spent more than two hours in it. He picked me up there once, taking me to church for a rehearsal for my cousin's wedding. For a few minutes, we sat in his station wagon without speaking. Then I got out of the car and went into the church. After a while, my boyfriend and I moved into a railroad flat on Alter Road on the second floor. We drank a lot of beer and pepsi cola. The empty bottles were lined up in rows in the back hallway. I would walk down the street to catch the Jefferson bus downtown for my job in an insurance company, wearing lime green high heels and kicking the leaves all over the pavement.

☐

When the snow came, I packed up my things and moved in with my girlfriend in the apartment behind ours. Her husband was in Vietnam, she had a little baby who cried all the time, and I was crying too over my first lover who was sweaty and sexual with someone else in the same bed where we had slept together. A life that is bound up with passion is a life of suffering. So said the Buddha, but I couldn't hear him whispering across the centuries. So I climbed into a new young man's car, and discovered instead that sex is an ever available age old temporary cure for sadness.

☐

For a brief time, I lived upstairs in a pink house with aluminum siding near the race track, not too far from where I worked as a secretary in a data processing department for a chain of supermarkets. I spent one hundred dollars on a 1958 grey Plymouth to drive down Dequindre

Avenue, in a mini skirt, listening to Paul McCartney sing about the sun. Everyday I'd walk down the street and back to the dirt driveway where my car was parked. Lots of wild grass and small trees around the modest little houses.

☐

Back to the city where steam is released from manhole covers, where my grandmother raised my mother and her eight brothers and sisters, where trees are tall, old and shady, on the dividing line between the well-to-do in Grosse Pointe and the ordinary everyday struggling dime store shopper, into a one bedroom with a built in ironing board and a boyfriend with an everyday two times a day sexual practice and a boat—the wind, the sky and the spray of the Detroit River heading north into Lake St. Clair.

☐

A new apartment with plate glass windows, trimmed lawns and a garbage disposal. Just as in the soap operas, I discover him with another woman. The sky is blue and my brother comes home from the VA hospital after Vietnam. I take a bubble bath, smoke his marijuana, cry more than a little, and then pack up my things and move back to the city, buy a 125 Honda motorcycle and trail along behind my brother and his friends on their Harley's. The wind in my face. Mushrooms and mescaline, dancing to rock and roll, camping in the wilderness, mingling legs and arms—a crazy dance to see and feel differently and quickly before those with power finally and emphatically delegate the trees and our lives to the museums.

☐

If when you look down at the ground, you look long enough, there will always be something amazing that you have never seen before. You simply need to look closely. I looked down and then I went home and started reading again, poetry and Victorian novels. I moved near the university, took piano and drawing lessons, studied literature, and wrote poetry. I heard a voice as I walked down Woodward Avenue, and it was my own.

☐

At Cobb's Corner Bar, a hippy bartender with a long red braid gave me a small beer and came home with me to my blue room on the third floor in an apartment shared with a girl named Shirley. His blue scull cap and dark red jacket were in perfect harmony with the color of the sky. I settled into the curve of his body for nine years, but one year and then two go by so quickly and what is new becomes what is almost gone.

☐

The French windows opened upon one of the oldest streets in Detroit. We'd drink and dance at noon or at two am, without drama, through spring, summer and fall. In the winter we moved into a big flat with many rooms, roommates, dogs, books and guitars. The branches on the big tree in front of the house were leafless, and many of the houses on the block were abandoned and in various states of disrepair. Ready fuel for the teenage firebugs. One day I took a long walk through the university and then I had a baby. She arrived without medical intervention, like a little bud falling off a tree in a storm.

☐

Around the corner, we bought a house on a land contract with a big full elm tree and a porch where we put a rocking chair. Bring me more books, our little girl demanded. A whirlwind of shopping, rocking and storytelling. One day I hid in the bathroom from the tantrum child who wouldn't go to sleep. I took a very long bath as I waited for another storm, another birth, a little boy who looked around, accepted us all—yes I have arrived in the proper place—and then he promptly fell asleep.

☐

Five years later, we sold the house, divided the money, and moved into our own apartments, the children going back and forth. Jump rope, trimmed edges, hopscotch, prickly shrubs. I left the window open one evening and a violent force slipped under the shrub and into the apartment, aiming for my back, and helping me remember every mistake I had ever made. When the police finished recording the details, we moved upstairs and then two blocks away into student housing. I started running one, then two miles a day, over the grass and the asphalt, under the trees and the gray-blue sky. My life was nothing like Emily Dickinson's except we both wrote poetry and at times we both were loaded and ready to shoot.

☐

When it seems as if there is no where else to go and nothing else to do, it is time to load up my car and move to a floor through on 8th Ave in Brooklyn. A seed carried away by the wind into the New York City sidewalk and subway system. The children arrive with their father. They don't like walking, they don't like it here, but he does and we try living together again as roommates in a big house in Brooklyn with trees, a yard and a dog. At night after the children are asleep and the AA meeting is over, Allen retreats to his room on the third floor, sometimes with a bottle of vodka. We are not good roommates. In the morning, the dog goes out the back door, and I watch the sun come up over the trees on Beverly Road.

☐

In a busier section of Brooklyn, the realtor shows me a small apartment on top of a bodega with a play area over some garages and with a tree sheltering a picnic table—we paint the wood paneling white and the children and I divide up the space. At night from the kitchen window, we watch the thieves ransack the cars on 13th Street and then pick up their drugs from the bodega downstairs. Fire crackers under a tree of Brooklyn. So I move again, across from the cemetery, working in the daytime and teaching at night. I am jogging around the graveyard, wondering about the bodies beneath the stones and the lives they led.

☐

We move into Allen's big apartment and he moves into a smaller one, six blocks away. The rain comes and the leaves fall down in clumps. He is yellow and irritable from his liver disease so the children stay with me. Little league baseball, modern dance lessons, graduations, birthday parties. We stand on the roof and watch the landscape of Brooklyn slope toward the East River and the Statue of Liberty.

☐

Near the library, I find a clean two bedroom apartment on a lower floor. Sixty four shelves of books. I am swimming every day. The children are here. The children are grown. The blinds are detective wooden and I'm following a man in a black hat, dreaming I am dying on a couch in a suburb of Detroit. At the point of an angle, the beginning of three miles of low hills and trees, we bicycle the surrounding avenues and crisscross pedestrian paths. At the point of an angle, black umbrellas enter the subway downtown. When an autumn leaf twirls to the ground, and the rain as well as a human shoe step upon it, an arrangement is left behind—stick, locust leaf, elm—a still life, for a second or maybe two.

☐

A one year sublet on the tenth floor, overlooking the Hudson. The wide sky, angular buildings, freighters passing by. Another one year sublet on the second floor, near the East River, all my books in the back room, white venetian blinds like my grandmother's, my big black bed, a wooden table and a desk. Looking out the window, I write poems on a manual typewriter. Allen begins to die and I go back and forth from the East Village to Brooklyn. An ancient practice. Open your hands and lift up your arms. Free that despairing, anxious ego and allow space into the back of your neck, your shoulders, your sit bones, the ends of your toes, the strings of seeds littering the sidewalks and streets, the branches and the clouds. Of course I always loved him. Each locust leaf has a life of its own. Don't ever forget me, he said.

☐

Peter Rabbit's house, my son says, that's what this apartment reminds me of. When he stands on his hands, his feet are neatly planted on the ceiling. Across the street, there's a park and some big old oak trees, some of the oldest trees in the city, the location of many punk rock band concerts, improv jazz sets, film shoots, political meetings, police actions and sunbathing Sundays. Around and around we go, circling the meadow and Krishna's tree, all those dog walks under the umbrella, under the shelter of the trees, scattering their divine and rather ordinary parts and pieces with the help of the sun, wind and rain, leaving so many found poems, in the storm or the calm, pointing—Hey, you. Look, look at me.

AERIAL VIEW

In half lotus on a hard mattress in a small room in the Pahara Ganj of Delhi—desire hijacked. Somewhere in the northern forests, the wind has an animal presence. I hold the towel over my breasts as if we don't know each other. An overhead fan puffs the dirty fiberglass curtains, slow and uneven, yellow flowers expanding in a small oval mirror inside a plastic frame. A candlelight vigil. Do not worry. You will be quite fine here in India, Madame. With descriptive scrutiny, a gaudy Ganapati twirls his trunk over the television screen, and the Russian lover who is no longer a lover scatters his clothes over the floor and his thick sleeping body on my silk scarf, the greater weight giving in to gravity. With no further training needed for sleep, get down from the pedestal of foreign policy, love him like a thorny rose, admire from afar.

☐

The crowd was coming up Broadway, crying and covered with grey dust. Thousands are presumed dead. As I hold a handkerchief over my face, the rickshaw slows down and then continues. I slip into sleep and then jerk back into a state of semi awareness. With the power of mind, body and speech, an old woman grabs my arm. Without any advance knowledge, we offer her the opportunity to leave with some of our food and she takes it. There's a big storm coming, synthetic dust, citizens, thunder and everything. The young Israelis huddle around their water pipes, listening to rave music, while the newscaster reports they are unable to calculate. Sometimes things are twisted for facility and pronunciation. While the rubble continues to smolder, we climb the stone steps of the great Delhi mosque. Immense black birds circle overhead, old men and women asleep on the steps, synthetic dust, my head covered with a scarf, a hankie over my face. A little boy stops me on the bottom step and asks if I am a Muslim woman. My children are already grown. Yes, we see a mountain, we see smoke and so we conclude there must be fire.

☐

So you want to go to Delhi but you have no facility except your legs or a bull and cart. It will take a long time. When the young rickshaw driver takes me all the way around Connaught Place to blow up the meter, he almost runs over a child. Beseiged. Then the toilet erupts and spews shit all over the bathroom. Tricked. Who are these unnamed enemies? *Aham Asmi.* Someone should be punished for this heinous crime. We are all stirred up with words, leaves, bricks and cement. *Manavaha*, a being who is mind dominant. At the little cart across the street, I buy laundry detergent and then begin to scrub the floor. A lizard crawls through the grating in the ceiling and starts dropping cigarette butts and little pieces of paper. *Devaha. Vrukshaha.* It is dusk and the window makes a shadow of a grid, with clothes hanging on a line at an angle, the dark fan cutting an X over the whole. I turn it on, the enormity of a blue plastic bag flying around, kind of beautiful, puffy and all over the room.

☐

I dream the children are children again. Take me where I asked you to take me, I yell at the man. Allen is coming over so I can go out. Quit following me, I yell at another man in the bazaar. I keep losing my ticket, stand up and hit my head on the window. Stupid me. Yes, churn is a very good British word. Now I can't remember the dream and he was so present, so alive. Misery is due to misjudgment. You are asleep and with sleep the object is deep darkness. Everything was arranged for him to watch the children but I kept getting the wrong ticket. These words are like dust or mud, pollution, confusion, so I couldn't leave and then I didn't need him to watch the children anymore. One must be trained to increase the capacity for sustaining damage. And so we are returning to the beginning again. A speck of light with no heat, like moonlight, hold it. Little are children, the dream I am.

☐

Thousands of years ago in India there was already an aerial view. Soon you too will be flying Hanuman. Anything can fly, you just sort of suspend yourself in the air from one position to the next. Without airport security, I flag down a rickshaw and begin the rocky journey back to Mathura. The surrounding drivers laugh as I make the form of a karate punch to hold them back. A hellish storm of ash, glass, smoke and leaping victims. He drives down the road about one third of a mile and then turns around with a sinister smile and says, "You give me 500 rupees." Without pretense to justice, somehow one side eventually gives in to the other, our bus stuck behind a large camel pulling a cart with four people, my shoes made from camel skin. A little child cuts across the busy highway. Millions of innocents do not travel after midnight. Beside me, two very skinny old men sit, wearing white dhotis, their heads wrapped with white cloth. The one on the aisle takes out a home roll and smokes it. The look on his face reminds me of Allen when he was dying—just looking out of my body as time passes, one small blade of grass.

☐

I wake at 5 am, lie still. Group, split, armed, solid, banish. Upstairs I am so tired again so I lay down and sleep for three hours, eat a papaya, drink water, sit here on the floor on my folded up mat with my back against the wall, trying to remember children, borders, dislodged, frenzy. I am very sleepy. Slept at night without sleeping pills, woke up several times, stayed in bed until 9 am, fell asleep and almost fell off the bed, woke up and moved into the middle. I am in bed for an hour or so. Fanaticism, backing, doubt, feeds, despair. I wake up in the morning, feeling rested. Ok now I need my afternoon nap. I wake up and I can't remember the dream. Obey, reactor, power, mock, cloud. I'm resting on the mat, listening to the singing. In the back room, it's so hot I don't know how I will get even one wink. Well, I'm going to sleep even though I can be observed here. Zero, ghastly, cat's out, spectacular, pools. I doze on a low table, intermittently watching the young woman wash and milk the cows. Two little calves frolic around in the dirt and dust. As we talk, we fan ourselves with little pieces of paper. She's interested in a love marriage, but her father is opposed. As I turn on my side, my body builds up a sweat from face to foot. Fire, nuclear, simulate, penalty, madmen. Then I turn on my back and the fan dries the sweat and I turn on my other side again and the same thing happens. Even though the window is open I'm near suffocation. Then I realize the fan isn't working so I crawl over in the dark and try the phone. It isn't working either. Senseless, drills, unimaginable, rogues, ripped. Then the fan comes on and I go back to sleep.

▢

Variability of the monsoon in India has made accurate prediction a very difficult proposition. In front of Ramakrishna, I prostrate myself. Ah, here I am. Don't kid me, he says, you didn't mean that. You just wanted to stretch out your spine. The fruit behind the leaf is only seen by those interested in finding it. Ever since Mihir was killed off in Episode 119 and then resurrected in Episode 144, viewers have been waiting with bated breath. Some friends of the hotel clerk had their child stolen from them. Four years later they were on a train and they saw their child begging. I find the platform and enter car 2A. Push ahead, he says, there's no order here. An organized racket involving sale of children as bonded laborers to factories in Uttar Pradesh and Bihar has been unearthed. The boy runs like an animal down the street, covered with filth, and when he sees me he dashes over with his hand outstretched. Those with a boat will be safer, crossing the ocean. Hello my friend. Then the female cat with one damaged eye stops by my table to beg. Two or three cows stand out in front. Little birds fly in and out of the windows. Security. Banish. Worry. Roar. Chance. Attack. Urgent. Radiation. Production. Handed over. Battlefield. When one dies, the soul is forcibly dragged, but today we set the bag of food next to a sleeping child. Resting on her haunches a little distance away, her mother scoots over and grabs it with a big smile.

☐

On the train, the woman has nothing to put under her head so I offer her my yoga mat. We all enter our disturbed or serene states of sleep. Recovering from heart surgery, she sleeps in the most undisturbed way, without casualties. I squish through the mud in my sandals to a dvd movie room in Dharmasala. Harvey Keitel in the back of the truck, all screwed up, wearing a dress. Kindness. They're playing American music so loud we can't talk. On its own soil, eighteen months ago she married a Kashmiri man and now they run an STD stand. Economic sanctions. The boy looks like he was picked up off a farm in the Midwest and dropped down into the middle of India without preparation. A criminologist in a large group will see the thief. Like a magnet, they find each other. He ducks into McDonalds and meets a very wealthy Indian man who takes him out to dinner. Indiscriminate destruction. His parents bought an insurance policy so if need be, they can remove him by helicopter from these mountains and take him safely back to Iowa. Free markets. Profit seeking. Heart stopping. Chasm. Uncertainty.

☐

I could write a book about losing my glasses. A young Indian girl in a torn blue dress begs for money. I'll buy you a chapatti, I say. No, I don't want chapatti, I want money. A banana? No. No food. I want money. Only food. Ok, then, I'll take chocolate. I want chocolate.

☐

A kilometer away from the village, in the heavy rain, we stop under a little tea shack with some other people. A pack of dogs joins us, one big one rubbing up against me to dry his coat and at the same time to push us over. We almost have a fight with the dogs. Hunt down and punish. If madness comes unexpectedly, there are hidden causes. We trudge through the mud and rain. Michah brushes against a bush and big welts appear on his arm. Nearby, the antidote looks like a lettuce leaf. He rubs it on his skin and the welts begin to disappear. The tall gravel mountains make a shadow, snow peak, a lone eagle hovering in the valley and then swooping off, the quantity of sorrow less in some materials. A monkey turns his butt and a young sadhu sticks out his tongue. Hashish. Last night the Israelis staying in the houses behind this hill had a knife fight with the Indians. All you need to do is sit as quietly and as still as possible. Carnage. Toppling. Collapse. Thwarted. Cancel. Tower. *Ram. Hari Rama. Hari Hari.*

☐

The Tibetan girls were tortured and made to stand all day with a piece of paper on their head and another between their legs. Five years of prison for ten minutes of protest. She escaped through Katmandu and then here to Dharmasala, but her parents have lost all their land as a result. The forces are armed, unaffected and incomprehensible. Plant

a coconut tree and those in the next generation are sure to receive the coconuts.

☐

Michah carries the green suitcase on top of his head, balanced with the others under his arms. You save a lot of money doing this, Mom. On the platform, families are curled up and resting on blankets. Beside me, a man wearing a turban stares at me. Civilian targets. Engine of globalization. I curl up on my yoga mat, facing the other direction and dose off. Wake with a jerk—is he really old enough to look after me? Twenty-two, ok, ok. The energy between child and parent is very strong whether they are on opposite sides of the planet or one is dead and the other alive. In the morning I wake up, open the curtains and watch the Indian flatlands pass by. Rogue states. Free markets. A baby who is sleeping beside his mother turns over with his thumb in his mouth and looks at me. I wave and then his eyes get very large. Aviation. Secret. Unexceptional. Cells. He turns over and stiffly closes his eyes, sleeping for half an hour more.

☐

It's because your skin is so so white, the boy says, and no one is used to seeing skin like yours. They can't help looking. I turn down the light. If it hasn't been resolved in this life, it is carried over to another. An American woman arrives at 3 am, lies down on her berth, reads a little and then turns off the light and promptly falls asleep. All night she does not turn over or make a sound. I know because I am up and down all night long. Under a cotton blanket, I dose, wake up, fall back asleep. The arrows in *The Ramayana* were like bombs, burning everything within miles. The monk who's sharing his bunk with the Tibetan girl, turns out to be someone she just met at the station. She's reading *Elle*. They are sharing one ticket. If it is inevitable to tell a lie, then lie. Two different men appear in the bunk above me to sleep at night but they never look at us or speak. It gets more and more desert like until finally we pass some barren volcanic looking mountains. To whom or with what. Destroy root and branch. Diminution. Then we pass into green land, a station and two little children standing under a water spigot, giggling.

☐

The cab driver almost has a BS degree but he had to stop to help his family. Because of his caste, he drives a taxi from 4 am until late at night. A curse for humans to work like machines. He's tired. I watch his eyes from Bangalore to Mysore. You are falling asleep! Buses swerve around us. No, no madam, only shielding the sun. Seeing incorrectly means seeing poison as food. Twisted revenge. Anxious. Security. Traumatic. Qualified. Possible. Airline safety. Resume normal life. Watch out, I yell, and we stop just short of hitting a bunch of rocks. Fragile and unfamiliar, the sky. Loss of records. I take off my shoes. In the path, one girl combs and braids the other's hair, so long, down to her knees. Leaving the body is as natural as taking a dress on and off. The teacher stands in the doorway, wearing a white dhohti and a long sleeve sheer white shirt. Anxious. Security. Traumatic. Qualified. Possible. For the time being, he says, your obligations are mine.

☐

Coconut oil footprints across the living room floor. The world trade center in its pre-attack splendor. I tell myself: don't be supercilious, but the tourists seem so vacant and shallow. Outside, it starts pouring. Sometimes I have to remind myself, westerners *are* human beings. All planes on the ground are immediately barred from taking off. I look out the door and think, this is monsoon. The US goes into gridlock. Texas postpones an execution. The young boy who walks the German shepherd shows me some scars on his arms from dog bites. You wander here and there along with your dog. A little knock on my door, and there is the quiet guru, in his white cloth, soaking wet. No towel. No thank you. Cotton is a conductor of energy. The smallest dot greater even than the sky. Only split-screen images capture the magnitude. When the priest touches my forehead with a dot of red powder, a giant stone Hanuman holds up his torch.

☐

I look up from scrubbing a pot. Duke is standing on his hind legs with his front paws on the window ledge, studying me with his glassy blue eyes. I toss him an almond which he leaps into the air to catch. When the bow is pulled, the results come. I was riding the scooter very fast when the weather dropped. I could feel it right through my blouse. Global slowdown. Battered retreat. Hour of silence. People perish. Water's filling up the streets. I'm very time conscious. Soon, you will forget the whole world.

☐

A giant moth in the kitchen. Tropical insects larger here even though the people are smaller. Roberto runs out of the house in his underwear, throwing a pot of water on the noisy children who are begging and banging drums at the gate. They run away laughing and then one catches my eye. He flies out of the house again with a broom and off they go. These motorcycles always remind me of large house flies from outer space. A wonderful machine, but irreparable at some point. Keep your shoes on, dear, the floors are so cold. The US is a beautiful country, blanketed with bits of paper, drifting, falling to

Cities and Memory 124

earth, a tattered resume. I can't leave India for a number of years if I want to stay straight. It almost feels as if I'm holding on to nothing. Check number 37546. He doesn't know when he's returning but he is sure to return.

☐

We have lost our capacity, so we don't see in the back of the dark cell, a musty deity. I step backwards past the large column which is constructed from stone plates stacked on top of each other. Before we had a huge memory. An owl can see in the dark. He will be invisible to others, existing but not seen. Watch out, don't step on Ganapati. The woman in the elegant red sari clearly does not like the fact that I, a foreigner, am standing beside her. Even a great scientist is a poor man, understanding only one angle. The young boy hangs on the side of the van with the door open and his face in the wind. Wall street. Big deals. Long term leases. Out of market. Rendered useless. End of the day. Demolished. Collateral damage. You only know you are dreaming when you wake up. Sitting here at this desk with the cool breeze coming through the window grates, while the leaves from the coconut tree wave and the man walking by with the blankets on his head, yells something in Kanada, something like yapurr yapurr.

☐

Speeding around KR circle, we stop on a dime, a few inches away from an old man wearing a white shawl and a dhoti. He turns his head, sees us with our western faces and our helmets and he smiles. Oil your body so you are not caught in a spider web. Then we recite the Sanskrit alphabet—*ah ahh, ee, eee, oo, ooo. re, roo*. No progress without memorization. I'm coughing from the cold air, red dust and diesel fuel pumping out the rickshaws and lorries. Press his shoulder when I want

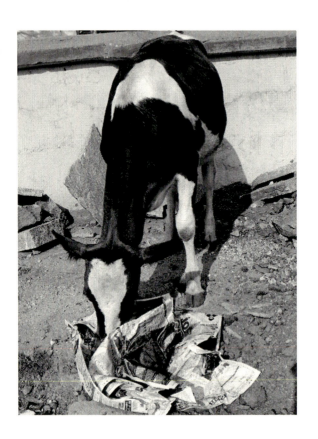

him to brake. Everyone is a tool of someone else. A cow lies peacefully in the middle of traffic, chewing her cud and looking at all of us as if we are crazy little flies. If three people pull a rope in each of their own directions— evacuation, collapse, technological disaster, blocked and herded, asymmetry of suffering.

☐

Indians don't believe that anyone has ever walked on the moon. Americans staged it in a desert and money was made. Post traumatic. Personal security. Anxiety. Rapid increase. I step over the woman doing the dishes on the floor. Don't step on red ants, they are vicious. A turquoise plaid lunghi tied around his hips, a copper band around his arm—Oh, ma, he says, hanging from two ropes and following the lines of my nadis with his feet. Out the window, the long leaves of a tree. They stay here in earth's atmosphere for thousands of years. Laying flat on the floor with my arms extended outward like a T. A cement rolling pin. I am a chapatti, all imperfections removed. Break through. Scrape off a thin layer. A human foot.

☐

To sit on a mat or scarf would be too ordinary Indian. That's where the British first landed. Hidden causes cannot be eliminated so easily. Let your violence be meaningful. A small ferry takes us across the bay and back again, past the giant ships toward the sprawling city with the cloud of pollution. Sprayed with brown water. Wearing baggy shirts so the men will stop staring at her breasts. Mahalaxmi. Female deities bring worldly pleasure. Bollywood. The breeze through the window, along with the sounds of sea birds and the pigeons of Colaba. They gather in the trees and argue all day long. One might need love of brother, but no delicious foods or close friends. Caste aside. Mangled.

Singed. Unfortunate. Unlucky. The Taj Mahal Hotel is so marble and magnificent. In their bookstore, I buy a book about the Bandit Queen—Phoolan.

☐

In California, Muslim women in head scarves have been advised to stay indoors. I could see the outline of his face in the dark. Choreographed. Rescue. Demoliton. The floor was swelling with breath and energy. Goruda's eye is so sensitive that it can grasp minute material while flying. I instruct myself to move back to the standard point of concentration. I'm very prudent, he says. Hallowness here and there. Cut off. High Speed. Wall. Before the computer age, I bought thousands of dollars of traveler's checks and two days later reported that they had been accidentally destroyed. Within twenty four hours I would cash the replacement checks and the originals. Extra technology is required to change one's caste. Now I have turned over a new leaf. The need to tell the truth as factually and clearly as possible. Earth moving. Heavy equipment. If my wife doesn't come, we should get married and I'll take you to these islands off the coast of Africa and we'll live there. Repent your mistakes and then forget them.

☐

Street laws are just gestures here. I was nervous when they told us to get off the plane because I look like a terrorist. When they pull her over, she says wait a minute, turns around and takes off while two policemen run after her on foot. The eyeball will move naturally. Some techniques are shy by nature. Madam you are not supposed to ride with three on a scooter. It's illegal. Why then is it ok for an entire family of five as well as a cow? Many will see them as mad, a little peculiar. She's screaming at the policeman—Racial profiling. I move her over to the other side of the road. One leg in one boat and one in another: you will surely drown. The technician doesn't wear plastic gloves or use antiseptic soap. What you start, complete. That is enough, you will be taken there. 200,000 tons of steel. 43,600 windows. Unadorned profile. The loose hairs on my head are blowing in my eyes.

☐

I put my glasses in my bag and then turn to face the mother guru, her hair disheveled and her right cheek bruised. When love comes in a flood, then no disturbance from touch. Poor woman, I think, as I am wiped down and thrust into her arms. She chants something, it starts with a "d". I am dizzy. The Indian woman who was behind me is now on her knees, gripping the mother's robe and screaming. If a female is healthy, her spark is downward. They try to pry her loose, but she fights them, scratching and biting. Daisy chains. One of the male devotees leans over and whispers something in the mother's ear. She elbows him, reaches back into the pan full of flowers, takes a handful and stuffs them into his mouth. Accountable. Heartfelt ideas are better carried by oral expression. After the entourage parades off the stage and down the center of the tent, a young blonde woman remains, on her hands and knees, kissing every square inch of her guru's lotus leaf pillow.

☐

In the book, the character died from typhoid fever in 1913. Remnants. Fragile and unfamiliar. Rescue effort. Retaliation. I sit on a rock outside the hospital waiting for my antibiotics, my head hurting so much that the skin on the top is sore. Yes, you are proud of your over activity, but in a corner of your mind, there is a depression. Inside the mosquito net, it is dark and I am frightened, my limbs locked inside a man's muscular arms and legs. I am going to put a bag over your head, he says. I gather all my energy, open my mouth to bite him, and as my teeth come smashing against each other, I wake up alone, hair matted and wet, shaking, 96 degrees. Try to know who you are. Oh, God. Fissure. Backlash. Sacrifice. Catastrophic. Then I dream of Allen, alive but ill, lying in bed with no shirt on. I am stroking the sides of his chest and telling him how much I love him. In the morning, I wake up with a head ache and no fever. Even though you are sick, you should keep your mind the same as before. There is a nightingale calling from the tree across the street. Hear the sound. A pure *pa pa pa* coming from the heart chakra. I sing them up and down. *Sar ri ga ma pa da ni sa. Sa ni da pa ma ga ri sa*

☐

Behind me, Dawn arranges her cane and her rather frail body. It's still dark. We're the only scooter on the road. A lone truck and some men on bicycles carrying heavy sacks. The rise and fall of races and cultures. Credit unavailable. Financial markets closed. We turn left three times, and then right on an unfamiliar dirt road. The quiet teacher speeds into the darkness with a foreknowledge of the holes we can't see. Collapsing buildings. Work teams. Demolition. Call it destiny or collective soul. Around Chamundi Hill, down another narrow dirt path and then across a field of clumps, rocks, bumps and suddenly a big hill. Possible assassinations. A drumbeat. History circles. I hold my breath and anticipate tumbling around with the scooter. This is it, he says. A straw hut on the verge of collapse. There is the problem of the shepherds opening the gate and letting their herds eat all our plants and trees. A cinderblock house with a cow dung floor where we meditate. The eternal beggar waiting for the opening of the door. Over there the school will be built. The sound of birds. Dew. The morning light is purple. I am chilled to the bone. Like a Steve McQueen movie, Dawn says, as we angle out of the field and then back on the road home.

☐

A man selling flowers wraps some jasmine in a banana leaf and ties a small piece around my wrist. On the outskirts of Mysore, many grand houses, and every so often a little line of peasant huts. The wealthy need their servants. Arrows. Here is the receiver. There is the sender. Shiva knows when it is necessary to destroy. I throw open the windows to let in the light. Dawn arrives, dressed in white, her blue eyes sparkling, one of the thinnest women I've ever seen. While attempting to sit down, she falls over and lands on her knees. You should wear knee pads, I say. When the gravitational force is cut because of upward energy, you will levitate in the air a little. Single action. Protracted. Bellicose. We think maybe they need something to happen so that they will better recognize the fragility of the system. Something will happen, no doubt as it happens to us all, she says, crawling across the room to spread out some jasmine and roses. If I continue to lose weight at the same rate I've lost weight here, by the end of the year I will have completely disappeared.

☐

I reach down and switch on reserve. Giant yellow trucks charge by with blasts of smoke and blaring horns. Sometimes according to your constitution, you must talk a little or go mad. I hug the edge of the road, cut through the intersections with caution and then zoom around the corner, past the Southern Star, the big public auditorium, the Pelican Pub, and the policeman at the intersection. One blink is the shortest period. In that small span of time, change occurs. I look in the mirror and see a young man on a motorcycle charging by on my right even though I have my arm extended to turn right. Now I'm on Gokulum road, passing over three big speed bumps and then turning left into a neighborhood of fruit and incense shops, metal ware, tea stalls and lots of people, cows, goats and dogs, crisscrossing and gathering along the edges of the street. Tight knot. Secret cells. Exceptional. Confusion. Armed. Dissent. Aftermath. There is a light in every material. I swerve around some holes, make a left past the two hospitals, go around the block and there is the temple of Shiva. He's sitting with Parvati and Ganesha, holding his three pronged spear.

☐

Blanked with bits of paper. Drifting. Falling to earth. A tattered resume. Miles away. Abrupt death. Mangled. Singed. Unfortunate. Unlucky. Outline. Aggressive. Stark choices. Prospect. Resounded. Talk. War. Single Action. Global Assault. Wall Street. Associated. Slams. Rendered. Useless. Square feet. Potential Loss. Demise. Aviation. Secret. Unexceptonal. Cells. Raids. Business. Personally. Barred. Light. Weak. Treasury bonds. Duck. Obituary. Tight knot. Forgive. Confusion. Dissent. Retaliation. Morgue. Blood. Increase. Aftermath. Anxious. Security. Traumatic. Qualified. Possible. Disruptions. 650 million pieces. Drumbeat. Assassinations. Overwhelmingly. Controversial. Looming. Cellular. Recorder. Dipped. Heavy equipment. Cleanup. Fires. Sectors. Body parts. Restore. Access. High speed. Extreme. Pushed. Suspect. Crack. Overthrow. Wind and dust. Flame and steel. The smell of human flesh burning. Arrows already sent from the bow. Anti-American. Anti-Muslim. Anti-Hindu. Anti-Buddhist. Eclipse.

You only know you are dreaming when you wake up. Two very large wasps fly around the bathroom, circling the overhead lamp. I open the window, turn off the light and shut the door. A cow lies peacefully in the middle of traffic. A pure pa from the heart chakra. Let your violence be. Twirling. The eternal beggar. Around a speck of light. Anything can fly. I sit cross-legged on the stoop and gaze west—it maybe a very long sleep—at the coconut and pomegranate trees and the sky red on the darkening horizon.

(2001)

CITIES AND MEMORY

> *The inferno of the living is not something that will be; if there is one, it is what is already here, the inferno where we live every day, that we form by being together. There are two ways to escape suffering it. The first is easy for many: accept the inferno and become such a part of it that you can no longer see it. The second is risky and demands constant vigilance and apprehension; seek and learn to recognize who and what, in the midst of the inferno, are not inferno, then make them endure, give them space.*
>
> Italo Calvino, *Invisible Cities*

When I was a seed half revealed, perhaps I imagined a cinderblock house, in a row of others, on the periphery of the city, halfway between Detroit and Mount Clemens, below and above, through the walls and towers, a karmic necessity, squatting down on the white side of Eight Mile Road for eighteen years. Lilacs bloom. A woman carefully winds her daughter's hair into little curls, pinning them neatly into rows. In the fall, apples drop and maple leaves gather in red and yellow. Three miles from Lake St. Claire with no mountains to tremble at the cleanliness, efficiency, quiet sidewalks, the blue lights of the televisions and the picture possibility even in hindsight that I might have easily found everything I desired and married some boy, some man and lived there for the rest of my life.

☐

Many houses go into the making. On the corner of Mack Avenue and Alter Road, a streetcar stop, a two-story flat, and my grandmother's flowered dress set apart for the protection of her nine children who branched out west and east and returned periodically for Sunday dinner and a stroll to the A & P, dime store and corner bar. Standing at the curb, my cousin and I play hitchhikers. The sum of all my wondering. A man pulls over in a big car just as my grandmother comes rushing down the steps. At night, I dream with the smell of yellowed wallpaper, the creaking sound of old wood, half-open blinds, and the lights from the cars and the buses splashing a world of shadows on the walls destined to crumble. The neon light at the gas station rotates 21¢ and the breeze carries a question—What are they doing? Where are they going?

☐

I'm on the bus in Detroit heading east in the dark from work to home, passing by the Jefferson Chrysler plant and the yellow windows in the bars and restaurants. For a certain lost grace in eighty-three, empty lots and boarded up buildings with an occasional brave soul walking by. In sixty-eight, I duck down in the passenger's seat of an old Plymouth. The police are on the riverside, the rioters on the other, shooting at each other and we pass unharmed in between. Blinking. Best not to fall in, linger over St. Jean burning, Twelfth Street leveled, Saigon burning. Communism. Capitalism. Racism. We are fighting that which we hold in common. A shotgun in the living room, loaded. At night break martial law and ring the red bell at an old house in Indian Village. I'm dancing in a blind play pool and fraternize pig, anarchy and disorder making a new order.

☐

The Corridor between General Motors and Masonic Temple. The inner center, art museum, library, Old Main. The imaginary city is the city hidden within, the like-minded anti-war counter-culture, the ordinary abiding place of the emperors. George singing opera at the

Del Rio. Over the edge, dancing to Bobby MacDonald on the piano at Cobb's Corner Bar. Taboo in a cocktail dress on the stage at Anderson Gardens. Crossed six, they fling him away, ducking down under the bar at Our Place while some guys shoot it out over a game of pool. Oblique movements. The wink of an eye. David, tattooed and ornery, signals me in for free. Shadowfax on stage. Reading the *New York Times* with the crowd on Sunday morning at Alvin's. Out in front of Né's elementary school in the car, listening to loud Motown sounds. Stomp dancing on Thanksgiving at the Unitarian. After hours, on the back of Gabe's bike, heading back to my place. Cass City was sociability revised. Each mind bears in his mind, the underworld, comradeship, intelligence, creation, danger, sometimes too much danger.

☐

Sally Young and her little girl pack up and drive to the East Village, and then we follow. The most densely populated island. A network of tunnels, yellow lights and intersecting stairs. We are walking up and down the avenues. The gravestones in the yard at St Marks at Second and Tenth. So many poems and eulogies in the ever ongoing take a slant and run with it. A dime bag at a window. Avenue ABC. Knock. Underground clubs. Knock. The homeless sheltered in the park. Knock them down. The police surround the square, spending more than the cost for housing. A student's photo of the war on my desk. Piles of bodies along the road between Basra and Kuwait City. Passersby and soldiers. Heads, legs, arms. Fast and furious. No chance to protest. The boat draws up, empty and good as new. Avenue B overnight pricey furniture stores and expensive restaurants. Kuwait City a new business hub. Giuliani and his guys do a number on rent stabilization. Rents go up and the World Trade Center comes down. Devastation. The rents go down for a day or two and then the war machine gears up, and we get talking, working and rushing around and whoa, trouble city has arrived. We discover that we will never be able to stop working no matter how old. In a rusty can, all have gone. Abundance for the well off.

☐

I remember sitting in an empty apartment in Brooklyn looking down at the buses and cars, the hardware store across the street, the café, the bodega. It was snowing outside and I was new in town. Walking toward the subway with snow on my collar. Then bicycling fast down the hills in Prospect Park, so fast that Linnee falls off her bike and never rides a bike again. On a bench in the Third Street Park sitting beside Lewis, his children and mine in a row on the swings. High and low. Black out. Where were you when the lights went out? On Third Street in front of the Hell's Angel's storefront talking to Lewis on my cell. Sylvia's passing through Tompkins Square at the same time I am. We meet in the center directly in front of the Krishna tree, across from where I used to live, and we hug each other. The line that separates the inside from the outside is constantly under revision. In the morning even in the desert you can hear the pigeons warbling.

☐

Passing through the swamps into New Orleans. Someone left the windows open and now the house is moldy. Michael buys a mattress and some candles and then we start cleaning. On Magazine Street in August, it is so hot I can barely breathe. A black man passes by and I nod. He looks down at his feet. Who am I? In the quarter, dinner at a restaurant with an excellent wine list, Café Mesparo, the original location of the slave exchange. Suddenly a brass band comes down the center aisle of—is it the Mermaid or Wanda's? Then a long bike ride across town to the museum in City Park. I am alone and Louis

Armstrong is on television, singing—Oh, what a wonderful world. At 3 am, on Canal Street a tall robust policeman is following us. I can barely remember the details, just the fear, and standing in a station for no reason at all. As I get older, I remember less. At the same time my memory fades, all the cells in the city transform, and then the hurricane breaks fast and furious. Bodies floating in the flood. Canal Street is a canal. Looters in styrofoam boats controlling downtown. An eclipse of the moon. The end of a gun barrel. Where is the national guard? Jets and helicopters overhead. Where is the Red Cross? The French Quarter has survived. Billions of dollars for rebuilding. The biggest rebuilding effort in the USA. And now everyone wants to move somewhere else, maybe Mexico.

☐

Borough of Kings. City of many villages. When you come up out of the subway at dusk, there are trees and people quietly heading home. Don't speak. Manhattan is still rattling. Upstairs on the fourth floor Allen's cooking spaghetti for Michah, Linnée's at her friend's apartment on Eleventh Street and I'm sitting in Café Greenfield on Seventh Avenue writing in my journal. Or perhaps Allen is in Copy Cat, sitting on a stool below stacks and stacks of disorganized papers and envelopes, listening to Miles Davis. Ephemeral dreams. At the Methodist church on Sixth Avenue, Daniel Ortega speaks about Nicaragua. We're in the back pew. The FBI and secret service agents are outside and inside every door. Their black cars on the street. Down with U.S. Imperialists. Or maybe I'm in the front pew with Né and Mook, mourning Allen. The quiet beautiful rows of brownstones, two hundred thousand, one million, two million dollars each. A man passes across the window with a book in his hand, and the sixty-seven bus heads toward Flatbush and over to LIU.

☐

A city of palaces. When I walk out of the hotel lobby, I am on the other side of the globe, moving along with honking rickshaws and motorcycles, cows, goats, elephants, dogs, humans and whatever else on a maze of mostly unpaved side streets. Jasmine. Lotus. Rose. Golden yellow. Leaf of basil. In the dark, I'm perched on the back of Andrey's scooter as he swerves smoothly around Mysore palace. City of white lights. Offer to God, sandalwood, oil and camphor, tinge of red. A rickshaw swerves around a calf, grazing her side. A woman jumps out of the road, a red bus barreling through the intersection, colliding with a lorry on Ashoka Road. My son's leg broken in two places. Mangled. A dalit's house. Water strike. Deep-rooted corruption. It is enough to be a Mahout like my father. A garland. Sex workers and eunuchs. Karnataka music. Hindustani. For him music was God. Stay away from soothsayers, doomsday-callers and the astrologers. Global computer business coming soon to Mysore. Good for work, for money. All the things contained in the city are included in the design even these puffy little yellow flowers with no stems. Hastily in a whisper— Hey yoga, you take this. Good smell. Su gandhim. Threaded jasmine in your hair. I had come to find peace. To begin, Madame, merge your mind with the ONE and your scooter with the traffic.

☐

It's cold here, even wearing two jackets and a Russian hat, and I need an escort and a translator to shop for vegetables. Little Sasha's wearing a red coat and dancing with an umbrella. On the sidewalk, a big stocky woman in an old overcoat sells wool socks on a card table. A square enclosure with writers dressed in black, smoking cigarettes and reading poems in a language I can't decode. The escalator down to the subway is so deep. Put your camera away or the police will take it. Waiting in line to see Lenin's body. Don't speak now. We foresee the exceptions. The people under these stones are responsible for the death of millions. Leave the manslayer no city of refuge. The tall buildings are fortress like and ominous just as Stalin intended. A Russian Orthodox Church and MacDonald's on red square. Just as the American global political businessmen intended. Freedom. Andrey on television demonstrating advanced yoga poses. Beggars on the corner. Displaced and running a fever, my India visa renewed, pack up early, leave Moscow and return to safety under a mosquito net in Mysore.

☐

On a small boat, I cross the bay, leaving behind Elephanta Island, passing giant ships and approaching the sprawling city, brown water and miles of shanties, with a cloud of pollution overhead. Mumbai. Bombay. Bollywood. Gray sky. Thick air. The hotel room is very spacious with a big mission bed, a table to write on, a standing fan and a chest of drawers. Everything that suggests a breeze floats in the window. Colaba and the sounds of sea birds and pigeons. They uproot and gather in the trees outside the windows, arguing all day long. I lie on the bed in my slip, happy to have survived the long trip, at home in a city that seems a cross between London, New York and South India. The city roar that hails Lakshmi, Ram and Muhammad. At the moment I am resting, the city of Kabul is being transformed into rubble, tottering buildings, and half walls, beggar children everywhere. The city of poets. Once the capital of the Mughal Dynasty. 3,500 years old. Ravaged.

☐

A woman named Violet chatters about tarot cards, western lands and city lots. A year of drought. Public relation consultations for new age businesses in Santa Fe. Photos of an old man in the newspaper staring with disbelief at his street, outsiders and insiders attacking, murdering and looting. God-given Baghdad, circular city, circling into worldwide consciousness. The American Indians are lined up on the plaza selling precious stones and figurines to the tourists. I'm missing sociability and alienation, that little bit of NYC distance that brings the music of everyone busy doing what they're all doing. On public tv, a moment of silence for each dead US soldier. 600,000 plus dead Iraqi civilians, oil deals, military and re-construction contracts. A few people on a few corners yelling at each other. *Support our troops. Out of Iraq now.* Chilly here on the outskirts, high up in the clouds, the inevitability of sunspots. Sharpen your eyes. It'll take a couple of years to adjust to the altitude.

☐

Each city receives its form from the desert it opposes. The skyline in Tucson is jagged, four mountain ranges, a big beautiful blue eighty percent all day umbrella, tall swaying palm trees and graceful saguaros. Hot in the daytime and at night pink lightening storms. Then quiet darkness and the jasmine climbs the trellis, a botanical thread connecting one reality to another. Ten percent chance of rain today. The sound of military aircraft overhead. Eons ago an ocean bed. Then the rain pours out of the sky dramatically for twenty minutes in one neighborhood but not in another. Scattered flooding, the influx of those following the sun, and the sound of military aircraft overhead. A white line of smoke in the sky. Pedal a little further south, away from the university where the houses are smaller, a little closer to Mexico. Hot, dry and dusty. The roar of military aircraft overhead. The rush of traffic on Broadway. Errands and appointments. The gift of water. It will last only so long. For the time being, I'm here, arms working, legs working, coasting along on my bicycle on the edge of traffic.

☐

Outside the train window, grass, trees, houses. They grow taller and greyer until the city overcomes the vista and whoosh underground I go straight into Penn Station. Socks and shoes soaking wet. Even *The Confidence Man* is wet and falling apart. Water everywhere, all day long, for two days, dragging a heavy suitcase. Second Avenue Deli closed, a Hooters moving in. Little Esther's rent is higher than my monthly salary. Have trust the cosmopolitan man says. A sign in Cliff's kitchen: Do you really want to work at Sardi's in December? I do not wish your eyes to catch a distorted image. On the corners, smokers congregate and plot some kind of revolution. Under her wide-brimmed hat, Rosemary Mayer sits waiting for me at a table at Greek Delphi. I'm late. I'm running. I'm knocked around, I'm bumped. A network of wires and pipes. Standing outside 158 E. 7th Street, I look through the blinds at my once apartment, now a modeling agency with two guys in front of computer screens, talking on telephones. The leaves from the trees in Tompkins Square are drifting downward. They crunch under my feet. Up above, the sky and a little bit of blue.

ABOUT THE AUTHOR

BARBARA HENNING is the author of three novels, *Thirty Miles to Rosebud, You, Me and the Insects,* and *Black Lace.* Her books of poetry include *My Autobiography, Detective Sentences, Love Makes Thinking Dark,* and *Smoking in the Twilight Bar,* as well as numerous chapbooks and a series of photo-poem pamphlets. Barbara is a native Detroiter who lives in New York City and in Tucson, Arizona, teaching for Long Island University and Naropa University.

About Chax Press

Chax Press was founded in 1984 as a creator of handmade fine arts editions of literature, often with an inventive and playful sense of how the book arts might interact with innovative writing. Beginning in 1990 the press started to publish works in trade paperback editions, such as the current book. We currently occupy studio space, shared with the painter Cynthia Miller, in the Small Planet Bakery building at the north side of downtown Tucson, Arizona. Recent and forthcoming books by Alice Notley, Mark Weiss, Charles Bernstein, Anne Waldman, Linh Dinh, Tenney Nathanson, and many more, may be found on our web site at chax.org.

Chax Press projects are supported by the Tucson Pima Arts Council, by the Arizona Commission on the Arts (with funding from the State of Arizona and the National Endowment for the Arts), by The Southwestern Foundation, and by many individual donors who keep us at work at the edges of contemporary literature through their generosity, friendship, and good spirits.

This book is set in John Baskerville's eponymous typeface in 11 point size. Composition and design in Adobe InDesign. Cover photo and all other photos by Barbara Henning.